The Women Who Made the Quilt

Ann Sargent
Bonnie Mettler
Connie Sidebottom
Diane Giberson
Sharron Carleton
Louise Spangler
Sarah Wolfe
Wilma Albrecht
Cindy Wilber
Andrea Holman Burt
Anna Stout
Miriam Nixon
Olga Acar
Marianne Yucel
Jeanette Arakawa

Beatrice Wright
Hattie Kelly
Cosette Dudley
Vernell Halsell
Eva Wray
Lacy Thornton
Cindy Wolgast
Terri Esther
Genny Pilgrim Guracar
Jody Gordon
Shirley Cahn
Sandra Hamilton
Mary Hyman
Eileen Gray
Leona Miles

Evelyn Chaney
Lolly Font
Ellen Tims
Bea Keesey
Connie Yu
Donna Oden
Connie Lillie
Becky Sarah
Soozee Becker
Marge Murphy
Karen Couzens
Vivean Andreas
Trudy Reagon
Karen Mae

1976 version printed by UP PRESS, East Palo Alto, CA

Photographs of the making of the quilt were taken by Becky Sarah, 1975 – 1976.
Photograph on page 3, right, by Terri Esther, 1976.

Color photography of the quilt for this book is by Dave Kostelnik, through arrangement with the International Quilt Study Center & Museum, 2009.

The People's Bicentennial Quilt was donated in 2007 to the International Quilt Study Center & Museum by the Needle and Thread Arts Society represented by Genny Guracar.
The quilt is hand sewn, made of cotton pieces and measures 71 inches by 129 inches.

The International Quilt Study Center & Museum was founded in 1997 when native Nebraskans Ardis and Robert James donated their collection of nearly 950 quilts to the University of Nebraska-Lincoln. Their contribution became the centerpiece of what is now the largest publicly held quilt collection in the world.

Through private funds from the University of Nebraska Foundation and a lead gift from the James family, the center opened in its new location in 2008. The glass and brick "green" building houses more than 3000 quilts, as well as state-of-the-art research and storage space, and custom-crafted galleries. The new facility enhances the center's ability to pursue its mission: to collect, preserve, study, exhibit, and promote discovery of quilts and quiltmaking traditions from many cultures, countries, and times.

The International Quilt Study Center & Museum is an academic program of the Department of Textiles, Clothing and Design in the College of Education and Human Sciences at UNL. The department offers a unique masters degree in Textile History with a quilt studies emphasis, which is the only program of its kind in the world.

Table of Contents

Genny Guracar, coordinator of the Bicentennial Quilt, continues her cartoon work on her web site www.bulbul. com. She sends her monthly cartoon packets to unions in the United States and Canada. A collection of her cartoons appears in the book, *Drawing My Times, Cartoons by Bulbul, A Thirty Year Retrospective*. Her quilts have been exhibited at the annual Pacific International Quilt show in Santa Clara, California, for the past 10 years. She is working on a quilt celebrating citizen free speech.

Connie Young Yu has long been involved in historical projects and social activism. She is the author of *Chinatown, San José, USA*, published by History/San Jose, and numerous other writings. She is a trustee of the Hakone Foundation in Saratoga, California, and is currently working with the Chinese Historical Society of America on "At Liberty's Door," a series of exhibits and programs.

A Patchwork History, Revised

Genny Guracar, coordinator of the Bicentennial quilt project, and I talked for years about reprinting this book in color. The 1976 original, was an earnest but simple paperback with pictures in black and white, available at community gatherings when the quilt was shown. The text explained the history behind the individual squares, but it could not capture the vibrant images and brilliant symbolism that gave meaning to the stories. In 2006 when Genny placed the quilt at the International Quilt Center in Lincoln, Nebraska, she realized a color edition was needed for those interested who would not have the opportunity to see the quilt. In March of this year Genny and I attended an overflow event at the Saratoga Historical Museum about John Brown, the abolitionist and heard his descendant, Alice Mecoy tell of how the quilt—with the Harper's Ferry square stitched by her grandmother, Bea Keesey—changed her life. And what did our California community have to do with the famous pre-Civil War uprising against slavery? John Brown's widow Mary Brown and daughter Sarah came West to live and are buried in the cemetery within walking distance of the museum. We had our impetus to revive the patchwork history; it was relevant, it had outreach and made connections between people today and America's past.

As I wrote in the old introduction, it was a cynical time, the Bicentennial. We were spiritually exhausted from the aftermath of an unnecessary, devastating war, the Watergate hearings, and revelations of our government's cover up and conspiracy against its people. The essays of 1976 evoke emotions of bitterness, despair and total distrust of the government. We were estranged from the national spirit, and we didn't feel much of a common heritage either. We put together this patchwork document of struggle and suffering and some horrific things that happened in America to people of color, to women, to dissidents, to immigrants and the poor. How did we ever think we were one people?

And are things any more optimistic now, with our financial institutions in collapse, the worse unemployment since the great Depression and our nation at war on two fronts? Yes, they are. While the nation is more diverse than ever, we are coming together as one people. Early this year we witnessed the inauguration of Barack H. Obama, the first African-American president in our nation's history. Despite the crises facing our nation, this transcendent moment cannot be denied. There are women who worked on this quilt who lived through the bloody battles fought over desegregation and the right of black people to vote. We never thought that in our lifetime we would see the dream of Martin Luther King Jr. come to fruition, and we who struggled for civil rights and justice would weep, rejoice and sing that we have overcome.

Our project of 1976 stemmed from an American tradition, women coming together to create from scraps of cloth something beautiful and whole. The quilt commemorated our nation's 200th birthday and in a sense we are a younger nation today. As common people speaking our minds and from our hearts, we no longer feel we are powerless and on the fringe of society, but part of the fabric of America, reshaping its identity and destiny. By our stories and handiwork we strive to fulfill the ideals and the dream of our nation, word by word, stitch by stitch.

Connie Young Yu, November 2009

The Quilt That Changed My Life

How could a quilt—a collection of intricately cut pieces of fabric, yards of batting, and thousands of tiny hand stitches—change a life? This quilt, The People's Bicentennial Quilt, changed my life by opening up a lifetime of research and discovery about my ancestors, my extended family, and me.

My grandmother, Beatrice Cook Keesey, loved to quilt. Some of my favorite memories are of sitting next to her at the quilting frame, attempting to make my stitches as small and neat as hers. While we quilted, Grandma and I chatted about many things, but the fact that John Brown, the 19th century abolitionist, was her great-grandfather never came up.

In 1974, unbeknownst to her family, Grandma participated in the creation of The People's Bicentennial Quilt. The forty-five squares, each created by a different woman, depicted historical events that shaped the evolution of America. The event Grandma chose to illustrate was the October 16, 1859, raid on the Harper's Ferry arsenal by her great-grandfather John Brown. My family and I were not aware of the quilt, and to this day, we have never seen the quilt.

The women who worked together on this quilt were both experienced and novice quilters. Once completed, the quilt was publicly displayed in 1976. A small article in the local paper mentioned the quilt display and the fact that one of the participants was a descendant of John Brown. Jean Libby, a university history teacher and John Brown scholar, read the article and contacted my grandmother for an interview and photograph session. The fact that Grandma remembered her own grandmother, John Brown's daughter, Annie Brown Adams, helped Jean to fully understand the importance of "continuity of history."

Jean arranged to photograph John Brown's great-great-great grandchildren: my brother James, and me. While photographing us, Jean talked about the "great old man" and asked if I was proud of my heritage. When she found out I was 16 and knew nothing about my famous ancestor, she spent time talking about my great ancestor, and started me on my great research adventure.

For nearly forty years, I have studied John Brown and my ancestors. I lecture on John Brown, his family and his fight for equality of all people. I have had the honor and pleasure of discussing "the old man" with some of America's most respected historians and authors. I regularly correspond with hundreds of people interested in my family—John Brown descendants, historians, authors, and laypeople. Every day my inbox contains multiple emails about John Brown and my family.

In October 2009, I had the opportunity to share the story of the quilt with hundreds of people at the sesquicentennial commemoration of the Raid at Harpers Ferry National Historical Park in West Virginia. Descendants of raiders, Harpers Ferry mayor and town folks, jurist and others connected to the historic event, including descendants of John Brown and his family, all came together to honor the memories of our ancestors. Descendants who proudly stood side-by-side 150 years after the infamous raid attended plays, lectures, music, walking tours and many other events.

A few years ago, I decided to try to locate this amazing quilt. Many phone calls and emails later I learned that the women who created the quilt donated it to the International Quilt Study Center & Museum in Nebraska. I hope that someday I will be able to go to Nebraska and see the quilt in person.

For more than half my life, I have told the story of this incredible quilt—the quilt that started it all for me, *the quilt that changed my life.*

Alice Keesey Mecoy,
great-great-great granddaughter of John Brown,
October 2009

Foreword to the People's Bicentennial Book

In the spring of 1974 a group of women of different races, backgrounds and political beliefs gathered over the commercialization of the Bicentennial and what we could do about it. We met at the invitation of Genny Guracar, a cartoonist and teacher of quilting. At a potluck in her home in Mountain View, we talked of making a Bicentennial quilt, a symbolic, tangible object of our nation's history. We resented having the American Revolution sold to us in "limited, luxurious editions" and plastic memorabilia. We were tired of being told by television commercials and politicians which were the "great moments" in our history, and what leaders and events we should be celebrating.

All our lives we've been fed history in which minority people's struggles have been omitted, in which women have been degraded, and imperialist conquest, and monopoly and militarism have been viewed as heroic. We wanted to portray the people as making history: the nameless, countless members of movements and struggles that have affected the soul and character of America. In this cynical time we felt there was much in our history that could unite and inspire us.

We began by making a list of incidents and movements most important to depict in our quilt. We sought to uncover events either hidden, forgotten or misrepresented. We wanted to show how women and men and children fought, suffered and died for rights and privileges we take for granted. While there are painful, harsh realities in our history, there are glorious triumphs and unflagging idealism throughout. We were determined to put together stories of what really happened to the American people in our two hundred year's history.

Many of us had never stitched or quilted before, but under the skillful guidance of Genny we learned both craft and history from one another. Each woman chose an important incident or movement to portray in a square, often one she felt close to or even took part. Some of us had ancestors who played a role in milestone events. As we worked we shared oral history. Bea Keesey, the great-granddaughter of John Brown, the famous abolitionist, stunned us all by passing around an old worn Bible carried by his son, Oliver. She recalled how her grandmother would look at what school texts said about the father and write "Not true!" on the margins. Some of the black women from East Palo Alto, Ellen Tims, Lacey Thorton, Evelyn Chaney, Leona Miles and Vernell Halsell, shared memories of their struggles for freedom and equal rights. Marge Murphy, who is white, recalled the Newark riot of 1967, when she was badly beaten by troopers while waiting with black people at a bus stop on her way to work. The man standing next to her was killed. She was shocked to read the distorted, racist press accounts afterwards of what had occurred. We discussed other incidents some of us had experienced which were misrepresented in the press and media. How will the truth of these matters ever be know?

History, after all, belongs to the people, and it will be up to us to pass it on to our children and succeeding generations.

When I volunteered to write the text for "a booklet" to go with the book, I envisioned my task as writing a brief explanation of each square. Instead I found myself plunging deeper and deeper into a mammoth research project that would change my perspective on American history for good. Each square represents a compelling story in itself, and as we worked, we saw how they all were interrelated and part of a whole cloth.

Since our first gathering took place, there have been major events for future historians to grapple with: Watergate, Nixon's resignation (leaving our nation for the first time with a president and vice president we didn't elect), the final withdrawal of the U.S. from Vietnam and Senate hearings on the F.B.I. and C.I.A. which exposed plots and conspiracies against civil rights, peace and women's movements. There are connections between our past and what is happening now. We have portrayed in our quilt the precedents of people's struggles and government cover-ups.

We hope to inspire other gatherings of people to celebrate American culture and history in a true revolutionary spirit. What we've covered in our Bicentennial quilt is far from being complete. But it's a beginning. A start in reclaiming our history and building on it.

Connie Young Yu, 1976

Negroes for Sale

...*We have in common with all other men a natural right to our freedoms without being depriv'd of them by our fellow men as we are as free-born Pepel and have never forfeited this Blessing by aney compact or agreement whatever, But we were unjustly dragged by the cruel hand of power from our dearest friends and sum of us stolen from the bosoms of our tender Parents and from a Populous Pleasant and plentiful country and brought hither to be made slaves for life in a Christian land.*

—from Petition for Freedom by Slaves, 1774

Twenty black people were brought to Virginia by a Dutch frigate to be sold as slaves over a year before the fabled occupants of the Mayflower set foot on Plymouth Rock. In 1670, Massachusetts passed a law proving that children of slaves could be sold into bondage. Slave codes were written into colonial law, and by the time the Declaration of Independence was signed, slavery was into its ninth generation in America. Washington and Jefferson owned slaves, as did many of our "founding fathers." The "peculiar institution" became part of American life.

Hundreds of thousands of slaves made the horrible "Middle Passage" to American and were crowded into the holds of ships, chained together. England dominated the slave trade, ships of the Royal African Company loading cargos of kidnapped blacks on the coast of Africa and selling the "black gold" in the New World. One ship would carry as many as 600 slaves, as traders tried to make a much profit as possible with each voyage. There was loss of lives with each shipment of slaves, many dying from disease, beatings, and lack of proper food and water. Black uprisings on the overcrowded ships made slavers resort to repressive, severely cruel measures. Two shiploads of blacks enroute to Charleston in 1807 starved themselves to death rather than be sold as slaves.

Slavery failed as an economic institution in the middle colonies, but southern colonies became dependent upon it. Crops that enriched these colonies—tobacco, rice, and cotton—were grown and harvested with slave labor. Black servants were needed to run large households on plantations. Said the Reverend Peter Fontaine in 1757, "…to live in Virginia without slaves is morally impossible."

In some southern colonies blacks outnumbered whites, but strict and brutal codes kept the white masters from being overcome or yielding rights to the slaves. Black codes varied from place to place, but basically slaves were not allowed to leave the plantation without permission of the master, they could not assemble without the presence of a white, they could not in any way conduct themselves as free men or women.

Blacks often rebelled against their masters or ran away, risking severe beatings or death. For petty offenses slaves were whipped, branded, or maimed. Young girls of thirteen or fourteen began to bear children, which were future profits for the slave-owners. Black women struggled to mother their children while either caring for their mistress' children in the households or laboring in the fields. Lemuel Sapington testified in 1839 to the plight of slave mothers in Maryland:

Among the gangs are often young women, who bring their children to the fields, and lay them in a fence corner, while they are at work, only being permitted to nurse them at the option of the overseer. When the child is three weeks old, a woman is considered in working order. I have seen a woman with her your child strapped to her back, laboring the whole day beside a man, perhaps the father of the child, and he is not permitted to give her any assistance, himself being under the whip.

Slaves had to get permission of the master to get married, and husband and wife were often separated by sale. Black families fiercely resisted division on the auction block. Josiah Henson, a slave who escaped to freedom, recalled the breaking up of his family by sale:

The crowd collected around the stand, the huddling up of negroes, the examination of muscle, teeth, the exhibitions of agility, the look of the auctioneer, the agony of my mother—I can shut my eyes and see them all.

My brothers and sisters were bid off first, one by one, while my mother, paralyzed by grief, held me by the hand. Her turn came, and she was bought by Isaac Riley of Montgomery County. Then I was offered to the assembled purchasers. My mother, half distracted with the thought of parting forever from all her children pushed through the crowd, while the bidding for me was going on, to the spot where Riley was standing. She fell at his feet, and clung to his knees, entreating him in tones that a mother could only command, to buy her baby as well as herself, and spare to her one, at least, of her little ones.

Will it, can it be believed that this man, thus appealed tom was capable of not merely turning a deaf ear to her supplication, but of disengaging himself from her with such violent blows and kicks, as to reduce her to the necessity of creeping out of his reach, and mingling the groan of bodily suffering with the sob of a breaking heart? As she crawled away from the brutal man, I heard her sob out, "Oh, Lord Jesus, how long, how long shall I suffer this way!" I must have been then between five and six years old. I seem to see and hear my poor weeping mother now. This was one of my earliest observations of men; an experience I only shared with thousands of my race.

The legacy of such tragedy, heartbreak, and human suffering haunts the descendants of slaves. For black Americans, bitterness and anger remain. For whites, there is a heritage of bigotry, guilt, and anguish. For all peoples in America, the early institution of human bondage is a root of continuing racial tension, violence, and strife to this day.

Indentured Servants

Run away from the Subscriber, the 4th day of November last, a Servant Woman, aged about 28 years, fair hair'd, want some of her Teeth before, a little deafith, named Susannah Wells, born near Biddleford, in England: She had on when she went away, a Callico Gown, with red Flowers, blue Stockings with Clocks, new Shoes, a quilted Petticoat, Plat Hat. Whoever secures said Servant, and delivers her to said Subscriber at Wilmington, or to Robert Dixon in Philadelphia, shall have Twenty-Five Shillings Reward, and reasonable Charges paid by Robert Dixon, or Thomas Downing. [Philadelphia December 4, 1740]

—ad in Pennsylvania newspaper

Susannah Wells, running away in a Calico Gown and Plat Hat, could have had many reasons for taking flight from her master. She was part of a cruel system that made her virtually a slave for 4–8 years or longer. Upon landing from England she was sold to the highest bidder who had her work to pay off the debt incurred by the passage to America. Still, Susannah was fortunate to have survived the many weeks' journey by ship which took the lives of many other passengers, either by disease such as smallpox, pneumonia, or influenza, or by starvation. Susannah could have been released from the poorhouse in London, or prison, or been from such an impoverished background that being indentured into a life in an unknown land seemed like a good deal to her. But the man who brought her may have been a cruel master taking advantage of her bondage to him. Her work many have been too much for her. If she was captured, she would surely be punished severely for running away.

Tens of thousands of English, Irish, German, and other European women and men contracted themselves to agents who paid for their passage, and they worked in servitude to pay off the debt. The system of indenturing men and woman was a way of solving the problems of labor desperately needed in the Colonies. It was also a means of replenishing the population diminished by disease and hard times. Some young boys were sold into bondage, kidnapped from their parents. Thousands endured the long ocean crossing, bad food, and epidemics to take a chance in the New World. Many who came under the system of indenture were convicts, runaway apprentices, prostituted women, as well as people who had lost their fortunes and wanted new lives. Many were escaping from a society where people were imprisoned or hanged for stealing food to survive.

Life in the American Colonies was difficult. Men and women, regardless of their class of background, were needed. A good portion of the population was indentured. Later on, after the Revolution, naturalization was meant only for "free, white persons," not indentured servants. But indentured servants face a good chance of working off this bondage in a few years and making their own home in America.

Many of the early Scottish and Irish peoples came as indentured servants, and were especially adaptable to frontier life and revolutionary politics. They formed strong anti-British sentiments and were active in the Revolution. Many indentured servants were craftspeople. From 1750 to 1775 twenty thousand servants went to Maryland, twenty thousand to Virginia, and perhaps twice as many went to Pennsylvania.

Early American colonialists were a mixed group of people, hardly aristocrats, a good many not even "free." The indentured servant came with as much hope for a letter life as an immigrant, and found times in American were indeed harder than expected. Poor Susannah Wells.

Immigration

Give me your huddled masses ..... yearning to breathe free.

Give me your tired, your poor, your huddled masses yearning to breathe free. Send…the homeless, tempest tossed to me. I lift my lamp beside the golden door!

—from "The new Colossus," by Emma Lazarus, inscribed at the Statue of Liberty monument

In the immigration station, I had my first surprise. I saw the steerage passengers handled by the officials like so many animals. Not a word of kindness, encouragement, to lighten the burden of tears that rest heavily on the newly arrived on American shores.
—Bartolomeo Vanzetti

To oppressed people throughout the world, America, a youthful energetic country of boundless recourses, represented the hope for the future. So they came, by the millions, first from England, Holland, Germany, Ireland, Scotland and the Scandinavian countries. As American fever spread in Western and Central Europe, millions more came from many other European countries. Most immigrants were young, and many were industrial workers, artisans, farmers, laborers, bringing new skills and expertise.

Not all found a warm welcome. One million three hundred thousand Irish Catholics came to the United Stated during the potato famine of 1845–6 and faced new obstacles. Better jobs advertised "Irish need not apply," and many Irish found themselves with little choice but to become laborers and servants. Jews escaping pogroms of Poland and Russia in the 1880s faced social segregation and various forms of discrimination. Italians were forced to live in crowed tenements of "Little Italy," and their labor was exploited in sweatshops and factories. Labor strife and the anti-Chinese movement on the west coast led Congress to pass the first major immigration law in 1882 excluding Chinese laborers and prohibiting Chinese from becoming citizens.

New immigrants from Southern and Central Europe and Mediterranean countries, and non-Christian immigrants from the Middle East caused a panic among those who regarded themselves bluebloods whose ancestors came on the Mayflower. Senator Henry Cabot Lodge in 1896 was a vigorous proponent of a bill requiring literacy tests, saying they would protect against "…wholesale infusion of races whose traditions and inheritances, whose thoughts and beliefs are wholly alien to ours and with whom we have never assimilated or even been associated in the past." The poet Thomas Bailey Aldrich decried the alien "menace":

O Liberty, white Goddess: is it well
To leave the gates unguarded?

The 1917 literacy test bill required that no alien over 16 years of age who could not read English or his own language could pass beyond Ellis Island. In the early 1920s, Congress adopted a national quota system. The Immigration Restriction Act of 1921 assigned each European country a quota. The National Origins Act of 1924 cut quotas further, and shut the door completely on Asian immigrants. Chinese immigrants suffered long detentions on Angel Island in San Francisco Bay, and many were deported.

Immigration was regulated to restore the "Nordic, white Anglo-Saxon Protestant" population. The Alien Law of 1918 was designed to exclude "radicals" and nonconformists who were viewed as potential threats, and also provided that aliens at any time after entering the United States who are considered "dangerous" be deported.

Immigrants came fleeing religious and political persecution, disaster and famine. They came in hope for a livelihood and a better future for their children. A good many did indeed find the promised land, and gave gladly of themselves to the progress of the country. Others were crushed by the new system. America, though a nation of immigrants, has never been a great "melting pot" as some would like to think. Our peoples have not blended harmoniously, and with each new group of immigrants, there has been hostility, hardship, and struggle.

Despite the abolishment of the national quota system in 1965, immigration is still manipulated for economic and political reasons. New immigrants continue to be exploited as a source of cheap labor. Prejudices against newcomers, particularly non-whites, remain. Still immigrants come from all around the globe, ever hopeful, and begin the struggle all over again.

The Boston Tea Party

This early incident in America's struggle for independence is arguably the most celebrated act of defiance in the nation's history, launching a revolutionary movement that changed the world.

In protesting the British oppression, colonialist organized economic boycotts and demonstrations. In a climactic incident that symbolized to Americans British tyranny, five colonialist were killed and several wounded by British soldiers in 1770. This was the "Boston Massacre" which enraged the populace and galvanized a movement. The first martyr of the revolution was Crispus Attucks, a black man, shot in this confrontation with the British.

In 1773, the East India Company, falling into financial difficulties, sent over a number of ships carrying tea to American ports. To Americans, who were avid tea drinkers, the tea represented British monopoly and interference with colonial trade and they stopped drinking it. The British ministry insisted that tea be taxed a duty of 3 pence a pound. This tax on tea, among other commodities, Americans regarded as taxation without representation, and they were determined to resist. Any American who tried to unload British tea or side with the king in this matter was dealt with harshly by revolutionary groups, and Tory sympathizers were threatened, beaten, and some were tarred and feathered.

In Boston, December 16, 1773, a group of fifty men roughly disguised as Indians boarded three ships in the harbor, broke open 340 chests of tea and dumped them in the bay. John Adams said of the Tea Party: "This is the most magnificent Movement of all. This is a Dignity, a Majesty, a Sublimity, in this last Effort of the Patriots that I great admire. The destruction of the Tea is so bold, so daring, so firm, intrepid, and inflexible, and it must have so important Consequences, and so lasting, that I cannot but consider it as an Epoch in History."

The Boston Tea Party was a daring, rebellious act that King George and the British Parliament was determined to punish. They enacted harsh, repressive measures that further angered the colonialists, spurring them on to full-scale revolution.

The Declaration of Independence: July 4, 1776

...We hold these truths to be self-evident that all men are created equal, that they are endowed by their Creator with certain unalienable Rights, that among these are Life, Liberty and the pursuit of Happiness...

The bells rang, the privateers fired the forts and batteries, the cannon were discharged, and every fact appeared joyful...the king's arms were taken down from the State House and every vestige of him from every place...and burnt...Thus ends royal authority in this State, and all the people shall say Amen.

—Abigail Adams, recording the reaction in Boston after the reading of the Declaration, 1776

Earlier that year Thomas Paine had written a pamphlet, Common Sense, which quickly sold more than 120,000 copies and eloquently expressed the need for immediate revolution. The people of the colonies were prepared to see the ideals in their hearts and minds put into action.

At the request of the Continental Congress thirty-three-year-old Thomas Jefferson drafted the Declaration with the help of Benjamin Franklin. The preamble stated the ideals of Americans, the right to revolution and to govern themselves—a radical new philosophy that shook the world.

The second part enumerates twenty-seven grievances against King George III, and the conclusion is a complete break with Britain, a formal declaration of war. In the early draft of the Declaration, Jefferson included an anti-slavery clause, accusing the King of dealing in slavery and not trying to prohibit the cruel institution in the colonies. The passage was ruled out by the southern delegation.

The Declaration was boldly signed by John Hancock, the President of the Second Continental Congress and fifty-five members of Congress, who pledged their lives, their fortunes and their sacred honor. Many feared that this act of treason would result in their hangings. Abraham Clark, delegate from New Jersey dryly remarked, "Perhaps our Congress will be executed on a high gallows."

The "Spirit of '76" as expressed in the Declaration inspired other revolutionaries around the world. Its radical principles were articulated in the French Declaration of the Rights of Man, and they also inspired Spanish colonies fighting the tyranny of Spain. Abolitionists later used these concepts in their struggle against slavery. The first successful revolution against a monarchy in a Western country inspired other peoples and struck fear in the hearts of many a despot and king.

Many, many years later on another continent a leader named Ho Chi Minh, in the struggle against French colonialism in 1945, read a Declaration of Independence of Vietnam to a crowd of thousands in Hanoi, beginning: "We hold these truths to be self-evident, all men are created equal. They are endowed by their Creator with certain inalienable Rights, among these are Life, Liberty and the Pursuit of Happiness."

Two hundred years after the signing of the Declaration of Independence, the document reads as bold and revolutionary as ever. Many Americans today would be afraid to sign the document.

The Bill of Rights

The basic freedoms of Americans are defined and protected by the first ten amendments to the Constitution known as the Bill of Rights. These amendments were proposed by members of Congress who argued that without specific guarantees the people and states would not be protected against government interference and violation of personal freedoms.

Adopted on December 15, 1791, the Bill of Rights has been the basis for law by which individuals and states have safeguarded their liberties. Minorities in America have struggled for nearly two hundred years to win the rights guaranteed in the Constitution. Political, racial and religious groups have fought persecution by evoking the Bill of Rights, and the struggle to exercise these rights continues today. The failure of the nation to live up to the Constitution and its amendments does not negate the ideals expressed in these documents. The hopes and dreams of a better America are still embodied in the founding doctrines of the republic.

This square depicts one of the freedoms guaranteed in the First Amendment, freedom of speech:

The fundamental freedoms that already existed in the U.S. are guaranteed. Congress is prohibited from establishing a religion, interfering with religious freedom, abridging freedom of speech or press or preventing peaceful assembly for the purpose of petitioning the government and seeking correction of grievances.

A United Farm Worker organizer once said, "Freedom of speech—we don't always get it, but it's an ideal we all have and we fight for it." Members of the Industrial Workers of the World, the "Wobblies" fought for free speech by exercising it. In some western states the First Amendment applied to everyone but the Wobblies and between 1907–1916 they engaged in about thirty major free speech fights. Wherever free speech was banned, they would hop a freight there and begin speaking. As soon as one Wobbly was arrested, another Wobbly would climb up on the soapbox and take his place. Some were dragged off the jail reading from the Declaration of Independence and the Bill of Rights. In many towns they won the right for anyone to speak to an assemblage on any subject.

In labor struggles, civil rights, and peace movements, the freedom of press, speech and assembly and petition were exercised and fought for. When a tenured Stanford professor, Bruce Franklin, was fired from his teaching post in 1972 because the university accused him of inciting students to riot, he based his defense on the First Amendment. Judge Louis D. Brandeis, over a half century earlier in the case of Whitney vs. California concluded:

The fact that speech is likely to result in some violence or destruction of property is not enough to justify its suppression. There must be the probability of serious injury to the state. Among free men, the deterrents ordinarily to be applied to prevent crime are education or punishment for violation of the law, not abridgements of the rights of free speech and assembly.

The American Civil Liberties Union is dedicated to upholding the First Amendment and since its founding in 1920 has defended the rights of individuals and groups to exercise our fundamental freedoms regardless of religion, politics or whatever.

Shay's Rebellion, 1786

In the ten years that followed the signing of the Declaration of Independence the nation suffered many growing pains. The new government was so weak that there was constant strife between the 13 states. Necessary taxes were not levied, commerce was unregulated, money was scarce and farmers could not sell their crops. People endured severe hardships during the period of postwar depression and many bartered for goods in order to survive. There was a loss of British trade. Importers and manufacturers demanded financial reforms and subsidies from Congress.

Yet 90 percent of Americans were farmers, many of them with small subsistence farms. When foreign troops had been withdrawn and the revolutionary army disbanded, the farmer lost most of his market. He found himself hounded for back interest by wartime creditors, and state legislatures began to raise taxes. Some farmers faced foreclosure. In some states paper money was issued, which soon became worthless. In Rhode Island some merchants refused to accept paper money, and the legislature passed a law whereby anyone who refused to accept the money would be found guilty of a crime without a jury trial and fined. This law was challenged by a butcher named John Weedon (Trevett vs. Weeden) and declared unconstitutional. In New Hampshire the military was called out to disperse a mob that had surrounded the meetinghouse demanding members issue paper money for relief. In Massachusetts the legislature ignored the pleas of farmers for easier credit and a halt to foreclosure and levied even higher taxes. On July 31, 1786, the legislature avoided the problems of the farmers and their possible protests by adjourning until the following January 31.

It was to these intolerable conditions that a Revolutionary War veteran, Danial Shays, responded. Shays, like many other farmers, had served bravely at Bunker Hill, and after the war became embittered by delays in army compensation, accumulation of debts and small returns for his labors at farming. The farmers had no voice in the state government. Discontented mobs attacked the civil courts where foreclosure proceedings were taking place, as well as criminal courts to prevent the trials of protestors.

Protest became insurrection when some 2,000 men under the leadership of Shays attempted to seize the arsenal at Springfield. A state militia financed by conservative merchants and landowners scattered Shays' forces at Springfield, and as Shays was regrouping, he and his followers were captured. Though sentenced to hang for treason, Shays and his men were eventually pardoned to avoid fostering more bitterness and precipitating further revolt. These veterans had protested their grievances, after all, in the tradition of the Revolution in which they participated.

Shays' Rebellion shook the nation and deeply disturbed conservatives who began to agitate for a stronger central government that would prevent such uprisings. The revolt was considered inspired by leftist elements, and even in the early days of the nation, was considered a threat to be eradicated. General Henry Knox wrote Washington there were 12,000–15,000 people in the country that held beliefs that would now be considered Communist, and warned: "Their creed is, that the property of the United States has been protected from the confiscation of Britain by the joint exertions of all and therefore ought to be common property of all."

Trail of Tears

During your 200 years of American Heritage, every tribe has had its own "Trail of Tears."

— Ken Powlas

The Declaration of Independence was not meant for the original dwellers of this continent. Native Americans were referred to in the document as "savages" even though they enabled many colonial groups to survive when they first arrived on the continent. The same year as the signing of the Declaration, the new Americans broke their first treaty with Indians, one of several hundred treaties to be subsequently violated.

During the administration of Andrew Jackson and Martin Van Buren, one of the most tragic phases in Indian history took place: the forced removal of more than 125,000 Indians from their homes in the Southeast, lands which became part of Georgia, Alabama, and Mississippi. In 1790 the government signed a treaty with Creek Indians in which the Indians ceded certain lands, but the government vowed to guarantee the remaining boundaries of the Creek Nation. In a war against the Creeks, 1813–1814, troops led by Andrew Jackson broke Creek resistance, and the Creeks were forced to cede two-thirds of their remaining lands. To Indians, the land was their mother, and they opposed the selling of their land, which was the giving up of their nation. The Shawnee Chief Tecumseh said, "Sell a country! Why not sell the air, the clouds, and the great sea…Did not the Great Spirit make them all for the use of his children?"

In 1830 Andrew Jackson, the hero of Horseshoe Bend, signed the Indian Removal Bill which gave him the power to initiate land exchanges with Indian nations. The Bill was aimed at evicting the powerful, intact nations of the Choctaw, Chickasaw, Cherokee, and Creeks. In November 1831, 4,000 Choctaw were forced to leave their territory, starting towards Arkansas in a bitterly cold winter. Their exodus was like a death march, with many dying from cold, hunger and cholera. Creeks, finding themselves invaded by greedy land speculators and bootleggers, finally accepted a removal treaty. Indians who resisted were marched off in chains.

The proud Cherokee nation held out the longest. Gold was discovered in their territories and greedy "land developers" were ready to take over. The state of Georgia passed laws aimed at negating the laws of the Cherokee Nation. The Cherokees sued the State of Georgia in the Supreme Court, but the Court held the opinion that Cherokees couldn't sue as they were not a nation in the foreign sense. In 1832 Samuel Worcester and Elizur Butler, Christian missionaries allowed themselves to be arrested for the crime of residing among Indians without a license. The case went to the Supreme Court, which found the acts of the state of Georgia in violation of treaties and the Constitution. John Marshall delivered the opinion with a vigorous denunciation of the wrongs perpetrated by Georgia upon the Indian people. While the Cherokees celebrated this favorable reversal, President Jackson refused to execute the decision of the court, saying, "John Marshall has made his decision, now let him enforce it."

History books have praised Jacksonian democracy, avoiding discussion of Jackson's hatred of and cruelty toward Indians. The *Pocket History of the United States* by Alan Nevins and Henry Steele Commager says of the seventh President: "Although Jackson's main creed can be summed up in a few phrases: faith in the common man; belief in political equality; belief in equal opportunity; hatred of monopoly, special privilege, and the intricacies of capitalistic finance." His creed, or course, was not applicable to the American Indian.

In December of 1835, Jacksonian policy forced the Cherokees to cede all their eastern lands. In the winter of 1838, the Cherokees, 13,000 men, women, and children set out on their "trail of tears." They were poorly clothed for the harsh winter, given the worse provisions and the soldiers served them spoiled food which made them sick. The aged and the children were the first to perish, and at the end of the long trek, one out of every four Indians has died along the way.

Even after the survivors had settled in Indian Territory under the agreement that their land never become part of the United States, their new home soon became part of the state of Oklahoma. Indians were the first victims of America's foreign policy, and "pacification" as a tool of genocide began with Jackson's administration. Education by missionaries, imprisonment in reservations and learning white man's ways by becoming white man's burden became the way of life forced upon Native Americans.

Nat Turner's Uprising

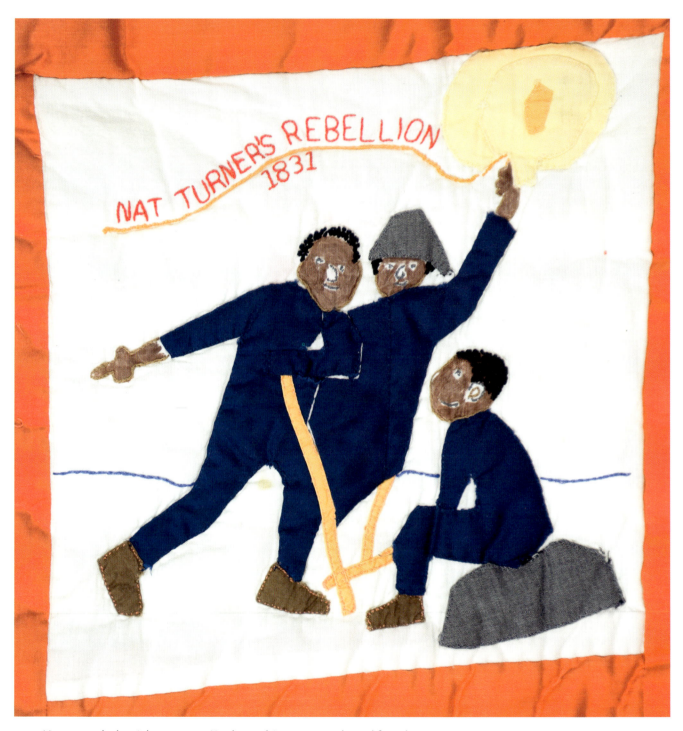

You mought be rich as cream/And you drive you coach and four-horse team,
But you can's keep the world from moverin' round/Nor Nat Turner from gainin' ground.
And you name mought be Caesar sure/And you got cannon can shoot a mile or more,
But you can't keep the world from moverin' round/Nor Nat Turner from gainin' ground.

— popular abolition song

There were slave rebellions since the beginning of that "peculiar institution." Slaves organized insurrections on the ships that brought them to America; many were executed or cruelly punished for rebelling. Slave uprisings took place which were more organized and led by more articulate and revolutionary men than Nat Turner. In 1800 Gabriel Prosser, after months of planning, led a group of fellow slaves to attach Richmond and seize the arsenal. He and his followers were captured and executed. In 1822 Denmark Vesey, who bought his own freedom, organized a slave rebellion in Charleston, but before his elaborate plot could be launched, he was betrayed by a privileged slave and executed along with scores of his followers.

Nat Turner's Rebellion was the best known of all slave uprisings because it resulted in the killing of whites, which outraged and terrified the South. A plowman and preacher, Nat Turner believed he was chosen by God to deliver his people from slavery. He convinced a small group of slaves of this divine mission and on August 21, 1831, he and his band killed his master and family and attacked other white homes in the Southampton County of Virginia. Within twenty-four hours about sixty whites were slaughtered. His followers soon numbered 60 or 70, and troops were called out to suppress the revolt. Over 100 slaves were killed by the militia whether or not they were involved in the insurrection. Nat Turner and his remaining followers were captured and hanged.

The South, stunned by the extent of Nat Turner's attack, responded with new and even more repressive Black Codes to discourage any new threats to the institution of slavery. Throughout southern counties, patrols and vigilante committees apprehended or assaulted black people they happened to encounter, searched dwellings for weapons, and dealt punishment to black people upon suspicion of conspiracy or causing disorder.

The Nat Turner uprising launched debates on slavery throughout the nation, and in the South, it dispelled any feelings of security among slaveholders.

The Underground Railroad

*Follow the drinking gourd/Follow the drinking gourd/For the old man is a-waiting
For to carry you to freedom/Follow the drinking gourd.*

—song of the Underground Railroad

Runaway slaves would look up in the sky for the Big Dipper, or the "drinking gourd" which pointed North, and on cloudy nights they would feel tree trunks for moss to find the northward direction to freedom. Black men, women and children would risk the severest punishments to escape bondage, running on foot, wading through swamps and streams to erase their scent and escape the pursuing bloodhounds.

Thousands of white families, in the South as well as North, at great risk to themselves, offered their homes to be used as "stations" for the Underground Railroad. Slaves would journey from one "station" to another, ten to twenty miles apart, traveling at night to avoid detection. Guided by a conductor, they would be hidden in barns, cellars, sheds, churches, in secret compartments of wagons and carts. The routes of the railroad ran from Southern plantations up rivers and valleys and across mountains to points on the Ohio or Mississippi River, to points in Pennsylvania, New Jersey, to the Great Lakes and beyond. Fugitives and their guides were often pursued up North by slave-owners and sheriffs. Whites caught helping blacks to escape were considered "slave-stealers," and they were imprisoned, fined and sometimes killed.

There were several thousand active workers in the Underground Railroad, and its vast interstate workers were well-organized and their identities kept secret. Some men and women did their part by raising funds needed for conveying black people to freedom. Railroad organizer Levi Coffin whose home in Newport, Indiana was a strategic station, helped over 3,000 slaves to escape. The courageous conductor, John Fairfield, son of a slave-holding family, used ingenious methods to help slaves make their way to safety, posing as a slave trader, a preacher or peddler. He risked his life many times and suffered as the fugitives suffered, from exposure and exhaustion. The most famous black conductor was Harriet Tubman who once said, "I nebber run my train off de track and I nebber lost a passenger." To raise needed funds for the Railroad, she would hire herself out as a domestic servant. After the Fugitive Slave Law of 1850, she took her charges all the way to Canada,

The activities of the Underground Railroad were extremely dangerous and against federal law, but thousands of Americans, men and women, black and white, from North and South, evangelists and atheists, believed in a higher law, and dedicated themselves to its work.

The Abolition Movement

Hell and despair are upon me, crack and again crack the marksmen,
I clutch the rails of the fence, my gore drips…
Agonies are one of my changes of garments.
I do not ask the wounded person how he feels,
I myself become the wounded person.

—from "Song of Myself" by Walt Whitman

The activists in the abolition movement were a courageous and determined group of men and women. The movement between 1830–1860 was organized by religious leaders and social reformers who believed slavery was unChristian and inhumane. Quakers had opposed slavery since its beginning in America. The black writer David Walker published his eloquent, fiery anti-slavery *Appeal* in 1829, stirring up debate and fanning the flames of abolition. In his essay, he called for militant action from his own people, declaring: "America is more our country than it is the whites'—we have enriched it with our *blood and tears*. The greatest riches in all America have arisen from our blood and tears; and they will drive us from our property and homes, which we have earned with our blood."

In the South abolitionists were regarded as dangerous outside agitators; in the North they were considered radicals. They suffered persecution, hardship and disappointment, but they continued to forge on. By 1840 about a quarter of a million people had joined the American Anti-Slavery Society with 2000 chapters throughout the country.

Abolitionist submitted petition after petition to Congress, but the "gag rule" of 1836 prevented the discussion of slavery petitions. John Quincy Adams as Congressman argued against the rule and persistently introduced anti-slavery petitions to the House.

Abolition meetings were broken up by rioters in Boston and New York, and in the South anyone suspected of being an abolitionist risked being tarred and feathered, beaten or killed. Publishers of anti-slavery papers were often assaulted and their presses destroyed. Elijah P Lovejoy had his presses smashed three times, and in 1837 when the fourth one arrived, he died fighting to protect it from the hands of a pro-slavery mob in Alton, Illinois.

When Prudence Crandall opened a school for black girls in Canterbury, Connecticut in 1832, the villagers tried to burn it down. She was arrested for the crime of teaching blacks to read and write and was convicted. Twenty years later Margaret Douglas was found guilty of the same "crime" in Norfolk, Virginia and spent a month in prison.

Lloyd Garrison was the most well-known abolitionist of his time and published *The Liberator*, most widely-read of the anti-slavery papers. When William C. Coffin, abolition leader, invited young Frederick Douglass, a fugitive slave to tell his story to an anti-slavery convention in 1841, Garrison was so moved he asked, "Have we been listening to a thing, a piece of property or a man?" The crowd responded, "A man, a man!" Douglass went on to become one of the most famous black spokespersons in history and founded an abolitionist paper directed at the blacks themselves called *The North Star*.

Like Sojourner Truth, the courageous, eloquent black women reformer, Douglass agitated for women's rights as well as abolition of slavery. Some abolition leaders could not reconcile their sexist views with the movement. In 1840 Lucretia Mott and several other women delegates were refused seats at the World's Anti-Slavery Convention in London. (Garrison and others boycotted the meeting.) When Mott, Lydia Marie Child and Maria Weston Chapman were elected to the executive committee of the Anti-Slavery Society, Lewis Tappan, an influential abolitionist said, "To put a woman on the committee with men is contrary to the usages of civilized society."

In 1852 Harriet Beecher Stowe's novel *Uncle Tom's Cabin* appeared, wakening more sympathy for the plight of the slave than any abolitionist propaganda. The issue of slavery was then popularized.

The work of abolitionists, black and white, influenced the thoughts of President Lincoln, drew battle lines for the Civil War, and finally led to the end of the most terrible American institution, slavery. After the war, their persistent agitation resulted in the Thirteenth, Fourteenth, and Fifteenth Amendments which guaranteed the rights of black people.

Seneca Falls

He has endeavored in every way that he could to destroy her confidence in her powers, to lesson her self-respect, and to make her willing to lead a dependent and abject life.

—from the Declaration, Seneca Falls, 1848

Two women active in abolition and reformist activities, Elizabeth Cady Stanton and Lucretia Mott, called a meeting to launch a campaign for women's rights. Several hundred women and some sympathetic men journeyed to Seneca Falls in upstate New York—and this was before the days of the transcontinental railroad, automobiles and the telephone.

At the convention, July 19–20, 1848, a Declaration of Independence for Women was drafted, which is as revolutionary as the document on which it was modeled. It stated: "When, in the course of human events, it becomes necessary for one portion of the family of man to assume among the people of the earth a position different than they have hitherto occupied…We hold these truths to be self-evident: That all men and women are created equal." The declaration carried a list of grievances caused by the tyranny of men, demanded the rights of citizenship, to vote, to own property in their names, to be able to acquire a good education, to enter any profession, to be treated as equals with men.

The meeting at Seneca Falls was so successful that it became a model for subsequent meetings and conventions on women's rights. The proclamation of 1848 is relevant today, and many American women have the same grievances so eloquently expressed by their mid-19th century sisters.

Sex prejudice has been the chief hindrance in the rapid advance of the women's rights movements to its present status, and it is still a stupendous obstacle to be overcome. This world taught women nothing skillful and then said her work was valueless. It permitted her no options and said she did not know how to think. It forbade her to speak in public, and said the sex had no orators. It denied her the schools, and said the sex had no genius. It robbed her of every vestige of responsibility, and then called her weak. It taught her that every pleasure must come as a favor for men, and when to gain it she decked herself in paint and fine feathers, as she had been taught to do, it called her vain.

—Carrie Chapman Catt, 1902

Harper's Ferry

It was sense of the wrongs which we have suffered that prompted the noble but unfortunate Captain John Brown and his associates to attempt to give freedom to a small number, at least, of those who are now held by cruel and unjust laws, and by no less cruel and unjust men. To this freedom they were entitled by every known principle of justice and humanity. Dear brother, could I die for a more noble cause?

—John Copeland, black student from Oberlin, who joined in Brown's raid on Harper's Ferry, writing to his brother while awaiting hanging, 1859

Letter to John Brown's wife, Mary Ann Brown

Farmer Centre, Ohio
November 14, 1859

My Dear Madam:

In an hour like this the common words of sympathy may seem like idle words, and yet I want to say something to you, the noble wife of the hero of the 19th century. Belonging to the race your dear husband reached forth his hand to assist I need not tell you that my sympathies are with you. I thank you for the brave words you have spoken. A republic that produces such a wife and mother may hope for better days. Our heart may grow more hopeful for humanity when it sees the sublime sacrifice it is about to receive from his hands. Not in vain has your dear husband periled all, if the martyrdom of one hero is worth more than the life of a million cowards. For the prison comes forth a shout of triumph over that power whose ethics are robbery of the feeble and oppression of the weak, the trophies of whose chivalry are a plundered cradle and a scourged and bleeding woman. Dear sister I thank you for the brave and noble words that you have spoken. Enclosed I send you a few dollars as a token of my gratitude reverence and love.

Yours Respectfully,

Frances Ellen Watkins
(a black schoolteacher and abolitionist)

At eight o'clock on Sunday evening, October 16, 1859, John Brown rose to his feet and said, "Men, get your arms. We will proceed to the Ferry."

Brown and his eighteen followers proceeded to the bridge—the federal arsenal was his goal, hoping the slaves would rally round him to disappear into the mountains. Harper's Ferry was the gateway to the swamps where he expected the liberated slaves to take refuge.

His plan failed and Brown was captured. He was sentenced to be hanged and on the morning of December 2, 1859, mounted the gallows, where he handed a guard two sentences written by him, "Charles Town, Virginia, 2 December 1859, I John Brown, am now quite *certain* that the crimes of this *guilty land* will never be purged *away* but with blood. I had, *as I now think vainly,* flattered myself that, without *very much* bloodshed, it might be done."

Three years after this incident, his wife, Mary Brown, with one son and three daughters, moved west to northern California. The son, Salmon, operated a sheep ranch in Humboldt County for a number of years before moving to Oregon where he lived the rest of his life. Mary and her daughters settled in Rohnerville in Humboldt County where their old home still stands. Annie, the eldest daughter of John and Mary, remained in the Humboldt area and is buried in the Rohnerville Pioneer Cemetery.

Mary and daughters Sarah and Ellen moved to Saratoga, California, where they lived out their lives, and are all buried in the Madronia Cemetery in Saratoga.

—Beatrice Cook Keesey,
Great-granddaughter of John Brown, 1975

Draft Riots, 1863

I've tried to get a wife, I tried to get a sub,
But what I next shall do now, really is the rub;
My money's almost gone and I am nearly daft!
Will someone tell what to do to get out of the draft?

—from "Disconsolate Conscript," protest song of the Civil War

On July 7, 1863, President Lincoln made a speech in which he declared that the Civil War is to quell "a gigantic Rebellion, at the bottom of which is an effort to overthrow the principle that all men are created equal." But the North had within its boundaries a great many people suffering from inequality and oppression and ready to rebel.

The Draft Act of March 1863 gave the president of the nation a power that he had never had before, that of determining the life and death of the men of any city, county or state. Many looked upon the bill as a violation of state constitutions. The Union army needed to keep its ranks filled, and all men between the ages of 20 and 45 were draftable. The clause creating the most hostility provided that any man could escape the draft by finding a substitute or paying an exemption fee of $300. The bill clearly favored the rich, and many poor Americans were furious.

In Holmes County, Ohio, some farmers took up arms and defied the draft law. In a battle with the Ohio infantry, two farmers were killed and several wounded. Pennsylvania, which sent more contingents than any other state, had draft riots in the coal counties that were suppressed by federal troops. When draft officers appeared in these areas, the hard-pressed miners, whose lives are already regulated by mine bosses, exploded in anger. The war had emphasized the harshness of their lives and the total helplessness they felt in determining their own destinies.

In some northern cities the protest against the draft erupted into racial violence with black people as the scapegoats. There were riots in Boston, Albany, and Chicago. In Detroit a black neighborhood was burned, and in Cleveland a hundred black people were killed by white mobs.

The worst draft riots were in New York, mid-July of 1863. They began when someone threw a rock through a window of a draft office at 3rd Avenue and 46th Street. An angry crowd overran the office, setting it on fire. Before long the entire block was burned to the ground. Angry whites, a large majority of whom were impoverished Irish workers, had little sympathy with the objectives of the war. They were frustrated by rising prices and increased unemployment. They saw rich men buy their way out of the draft while they were sent to fight a war that was going to liberate all Negroes. They feared being overrun by blacks who would take their jobs away. Any blacks who crossed the paths of the furious mobs were beaten or killed. Some blacks were hanged from lampposts. Police and anyone who tried to prevent the lynchings were beaten or killed. The authorities were badly outnumbered, so the riots raged for several days. Homes of blacks were burned, businesses employing blacks were looted and vandalized, and the mayor's house was attacked. The Colored Orphan Asylum was set on fire.

The Draft Act was suspended until the army arrived to restore order, and city authorities, in an effort to pacify the defiant mobs, announced that funds would be set aside for those too poor to pay the $300 commutation fee. The discrimination clause of the draft law was ended the following year. The extensive property damage and loss of human lives caused by violent and racist reaction to the first National Conscription Act cruelly demonstrated that the North had it own house to tend to.

Emancipation Proclamation

One of the most important documents in American history, it became a symbol for the moral force of the Union and defined the cause for which the North was fighting. Issued by Abraham Lincoln, it proclaimed as of January 1, 1863, slaves held in the rebellious states "henceforward shall be free." After two years of bloody civil war, the Emancipation Proclamation captured the hearts and minds of the American people and gave greater purpose to the Union Army.

It was a symbolic edit that inspired people even though it did not establish freedom for all slaves, only those in the states that seceded from the Union. Prior to the Proclamation, slaves in the South sought to free themselves, defying laws that declared them chattel. The white people who helped them were viewed as criminals by law. With the Emancipation Proclamation a great principal of human freedom was brought forth, even as the conflict intensified. It was also a political and military measure that strengthened the North, determining the freedom of slaves in southern states by Union victories and welcoming blacks into the Union Army. Lincoln, favoring gradual emancipation and colonization of blacks, did not use his presidential power to free slaves in areas under Union control. Many slaves in border states were not freed until the Thirteenth Amendment, passed on January 31, 1865, which abolished slavery everywhere in the United States.

Yet the Emancipation Proclamation changed the character of the war, making the Union forces a liberation army to black people. Lincoln, by this decree, determined for all that the high purpose of the fighting and sacrifice was to abolish slavery. The edict caused confusion in the South and deprived the Confederacy of needed manpower. To abolitionists, the Proclamation, although not embodying all they had worked for, presented new hope for government action in the cause of the winning freedom and equality for black people in America. On New Year's eve in 1862, the day before the Proclamation would take effect, black and white abolitionists throughout the country gathered in churches and meeting places to sing and celebrate the arrival of the "Year of Jubilee."

Chinese Labor on the Railroad

In the veins of our people, flows the commingled blood of the four greatest nationalities of modern days. The impetuous daring and dash of the French, the philosophical and sturdy spirit of the German, the unflinching solidity of the English, and the light-hearted impetuosity of the Irish, have all contributed each its appropriate share…A people deducing its origins from such races, and condensing their best traits into its national life, is capable of any achievement.

—Judge Nathaniel Bennett, keynote speaker at the Golden Spike Convention in San Francisco, 1869

"I worked on the Iron Road."
—Lee Wong Sang, Connie Young Yu's
great-grandfather

The building of the transcontinental railroad was an enormous accomplishment which united two portions of the United States by rail and was heralded as the "work of the age." Its successful completion was largely due to the skill and endurance of 12,000 Chinese Pacific workers who suffered incredible hardships during the building of the railroad.

The Union Pacific, coming from the East, also had a largely immigrant workforce, the thousands of exploited Irish, as well as Mormon crews of Utah. Union Pacific workers laid 1,086 miles of track, and the Central Pacific 690, but the latter company, having to cross the treacherous high Sierras, had a far more perilous and difficult course, and an unknown number of Chinese were killed during the several years' construction.

At Promontory, Utah, May 10, 1869, officials, politicians and townspeople gathered for the triumphant Golden Spike ceremony marking the "meeting of the rails." Neither praise nor recognition was given to the nameless thousands of Chinese workers who made up four-fifths of the work force of the Central Pacific which built the western portion of the railroad. They were excluded from the historic Golden Spike photographs, and their achievements are often forgotten in history. At the Centennial Ceremony of the Transcontinental Railroad in 1969 the keynote speaker, Secretary of Transportation John Volpe, asked rhetorically, "Who else but Americans could drill ten tunnels in mountains 30 feet deep in snow? Who else but Americans could chisel through miles of solid granite? Who else but Americans could have laid ten miles of track in 12 hours?"

Who else indeed but Chinese laborers who were denied civil rights, who were unequally taxed and excluded from public education and a variety of occupations, who were forbidden to become naturalized American citizens?

Chinese labor developed a good part of the western United States, and Chinese workers advanced agriculture, mining and many industries. Yet the history of Chinese immigration to America is one of struggle against discrimination, legalized and otherwise. Chinese is the only race excluded from immigration by name. The Burlingame Treaty of 1868 was forced upon China to ensure free flow of cheap labor. When labor unions saw Chinese as an economic threat and the fear of "yellow peril" spread, the government passed the Chinese Exclusion Law of 1882 which forbade the immigration of Chinese laborers and reaffirmed that no Chinese could be naturalized.

Racism institutionalized by law wrought untold suffering on Chinese pioneer and immigrant alike. Massacres of Chinese and burnings of Chinatowns were common in the latter part of the 19th century and by the 20th, the nation had established a tradition of discrimination against Asians. Angel Island in San Francisco Bay was the immigration station between 1910 and 1940 whereupon thousands of Chinese immigrants or returnees from China were detained for months and even years. Deportations of Chinese were common, and harassment was used to discourage immigration. The Chinese Exclusion Law was not repealed until 1943, when the U.S. and China were allies in WWII, but for decades after, the remnants of discrimination remained.

Even while building the railroad they struggled against blatant discrimination. In 1867 they went on strike over unfair treatment, declaring, "eight hours a day good enough for white man, good enough for Chinese too." The strike was dealt with harshly, and the Chinese were forced to return to the same workload.

Chinese did not submit to oppression without fighting back. They took their grievances to the streets and to the courts. Some of their civil rights victories set precedents which upheld the Constitution for all people.

Incident at Haymarket Square, Chicago

*We mean to make things over/We're tired of toil for nought
But bare enough to live on; never/An hour for thought.
We want to feel the sunshine: we/Want to smell the flowers
We're sure that God has willed it/And we mean to have eight hours.
We're summoning our forces from/Shipyard, shop and mill
Eight hours for work, eight hours for rest/Eight hours for what we will!*

—popular labor song of 1886

The forces of labor were gathering momentum, and the newly founded American Federation of Labor had passed a resolution calling all labor to join on May 1, 1886, to establish an eight-hour day. Industrialists looked with horror upon the growing labor movement and hoped to break its strength. Newspapers across the nation attacked labor and *The New York Times* declared the struggle for an eight-hour day "un-American" and that "labor disturbances are brought about by foreigners."

Tensions mounted in Chicago preceding the May 1st strike. Employers of the industrial center readied themselves with special police and Pinkertons, and the National Guards was mobilized, ready for violence.

But May 1st in Chicago was a proud celebration for workers. Eighty thousand people stopped work, and a huge parade of labor marched down Michigan Avenue. It was a peaceful demonstration and rally, and workers were jubilant, hopeful of success in winning the eight-hour day.

On May 3rd, a crowd of locked-out employees clashed with the police, and several workers were shot by the officers as they retreated. A rally was called for the following evening in Haymarket Square to protest police brutality and continue agitation for the eight-hour day.

One hundred and eighty police were called to keep watch on the rally. It was a peaceful demonstration, however, attended by the mayor of Chicago who was in the crowd watching for any disturbances. Albert Parsons, trade union organization, and August Spies, editor of a German worker' paper, were keynote speakers. When the rally was nearly over, the police marched on the demonstration, ordering the crowd to disperse. "But captain, we are peaceable," said a rally organizer. Then suddenly a bomb was thrown in the night. Police fired in the dark and struck at demonstrators with their clubs. Seven policemen were killed by the explosion, sixty-seven wounded. Four workers died and fifty more were injured.

The bomb-thrower was never found, and labor organizers were convinced that industrialists, determined to destroy the labor movement, were responsible. Newspapers spread lurid reports of labor's conspiracy to overthrow the country, making allegations that the speakers at the rally arranged the bomb-throwing. Police raided labor headquarters, arresting suspects and beating them. Foreign-language newspaper presses were smashed. Eight suspects, among them Albert Parsons and August Spies, were convicted of murdering the policemen at Haymarket.

Albert Parsons, whose wife and two young children accompanied him at the Haymarket rally, insisted that he never advocated violence, that he and his fellow workers were convicted of the crime of being labor organizers, that they were victims of a monopolist conspiracy. August Spies addressed the judge defiantly, "And if you think you can crush out those ideas that are gaining ground more and more every day, if you think you can crush them our by sending us to the gallows…if you would once more have people suffer the penalty of death because they have dared to tell the truth…then I will proudly and defiantly pay the costly price! Call your hangman!"

Persons, Spies, Adolf Fischer and George Engel (the last three called by the press "European conspirators" because they were immigrants) were hanged. Four others had life sentences. In 1893 the three surviving prisoners were pardoned by Governor Algeld of Illinois on grounds that they were not granted a fair trial. The widow of Parsons, Lucy Eldine Gonzales Parsons of Mexican-Indian heritage, who fought desperately to save her husband's life, continued to work in the labor movement and became a founder of the Industrial Workers of the World.

Newspapers and magazines spread public panic over socialists and anarchists, creating the stereotype of the violent bomb-throwing half-crazed alien, seeking to overthrow the country. American labor suffered a serious setback after the Haymarket incident, but the A.F. of L. continued to organize for the eight-hour day. May 1, 1890 was another landmark in the labor movement, and on that day workers all over the world joined in support of the shorter work day. The International May Day grew out of the struggle for the eight-hour day in America.

Wounded Knee

"In the 200 years of your American heritage, the Indian has suffered, and still does, from the capitalist, colonial tyranny imposed on him since the founding fathers ironically released themselves from their own oppressive colonial tyrants."
— Ken Powlas

Upon America's Centennial celebration the 7th Calvary, led by Custer, met a crushing defeat by the forces of Crazy Horse and Sitting Bull at the Battle of Little Big Horn. News of this incident appeared in the eastern papers on July 5th, 1876. The government, humiliated and vengeful, was determined to settle the "Indian problem" once and for all, launching a campaign of harassment, land theft and slaughter.

In desperation and despair over the loss of land and oppression by federal troops, the Plains Indians in 1889 adopted a religion called the Ghost Dance, a belief that the spirits of departed Indians would return to help the living, and Indians would again thrive in their own nations. As this religion spread quickly, the federal government, fearing an uprising, wanted the Ghost Dance stopped. The Indian Bureau in Washington blamed the great chief Sitting Bull for the agitation. He was arrested and subsequently assassinated.

Joined by some of Sitting Bull's tribe, Big Foot, the Hunkpapa Sioux chief, took his people to Pine Ridge, South Dakota to seek the protection of Chief Red Cloud. On the cold snowy trek they were arrested by a unit of the 7th Calvary with orders to take the Indians to an army camp on a creek known as Wounded Knee. Here the 120 men and 230 women and children were kept prisoner, encircled by troops with four Hotchkiss guns overlooking the camp, positioned on the Sioux teepees. The soldiers forced the Indians to turn in all their guns, knives, axes, and searched all their belongings. Then they ordered the Indians to remove their blankets to be searched further.

Indians and soldiers broke into a fight, and the shooting began. The huge machine guns on the hills opened fire on the camp, the barrage of bullets cutting down men, women and children. The soldiers pursued those who tried to escape the circle of fire, and some of the women were chased for miles before they were killed. On the fourth day after Christmas, 1890, three hundred Indians were massacred. Years later Black Elk recalled:

When I look back now from this high hill of my old age, I can see the butchered women and children lying heaped and scattered all along the crooked gulch as plain as when I saw them with eyes still young. And I can see that something else died there in the bloody mud, and was buried in the blizzard. A people's dream died there. It was a beautiful dream…the nation's hoop is broken and scattered. There is no center any longer and the scared tree is dead.

American Indians are written off in history as a tragic chapter of the past at best, while popular culture either perpetuates the image of the bloodthirsty, wild red man or as noble savages in a pageant of long ago. Yet the contemporary Indian is ignored.

When Native Americans took over Alcatraz in November of 1969, the nation was forced to face the reality of their grievances. Alcatraz became the symbol of the Indian movement to restore tribal lands, inspiring other activism. In 1972, a thousand Native Americans from many tribes joined a caravan known as the Trail of Broken Treaties to present the Twenty Points to the government, the most fundamental of the demands being the restoration of treaty relations. Some occupied the incompetent Bureau of Indian Affairs in Washington to make their case.

Eighty-three years after the bloody massacre at Wounded Knee, a new state of siege took place. Wounded Knee 1973 was a 73-day occupation by Indians protesting the recent murder of several of their people, loss of land, loss of tribal government and federal bungling of Indian affairs. The conditions of Pine Ridge reservation were typical of many reservations: an average yearly income of $1500 per family and 70 percent unemployment rate. AIM, the American Indian Movement, led by Russell Means and Dennis Banks, made Wounded Knee the scene of international attention. The village on Pine Ridge became a symbol of new self-determination for all Indians. The federal blockade of Wounded Knee and the ensuing battle resulting in two Indian deaths and the wounding of a U.S. Marshal caused national shame at a time when the U.S. was fighting a war against other small nations in Southeast Asia. Apparently, all "enemies" of the U.S. lived in villages.

Promises from the government made during recent Indian protests have not been kept, and Indians continue to struggle for survival. Many Indians were indicted for the 1973 occupation of Wounded Knee, but they and those they inspired by their symbolic actions are determined to win back rights originally recognized in treaties with the United States.

Pullman Strike

Remember we are workingmen, and we want honest pay.
And gentlemen, remember, we work hard day by day;
Let Pullman remember too, no matter where he roams,
We built up his capital, and we're pleading for our homes.

—from strike song, 1894

It was work and poverty in Pullmantown, or Pullmandown until patience ceasing to be a virtue and further forbearance becoming a treason to life, liberty and the pursuit of happiness. The employees determined to strike to better their conditions.

—Eugene Debs, addressing first annual convention of the American Railway Union, 1894

Pullman, Illinois was a "model community" where five thousand employees of George Pullman, inventor of the sleeping car, were forced to live. Pullman devised a system of getting back the meager wages he paid his workers by setting up the company town. The housing at Pullman was twenty-five percent higher than outside the town, and the utilities were several times higher. Workers had to shop at the company store. All at a huge profit to Pullman and his investors. If there was ever a clear case of corporate feudalism, it was at Pullman.

In the lean year of 1894, wages were cut so Pullman could keep up dividend payments to stockholders. When members of a worker committee who addressed their grievances to management were laid off, the workers voted to strike. Support came from the newly organized American Railway Union, whose president Eugene Debs had won respect from workers for his successful leadership of the strike against the Great Northern Railroad. Members of the A.R.U. voted not to handle Pullman cars in support of the strikers. Within a few weeks, transportation was paralyzed in half the country. The employers' organization, the General Managers' Association, desperate to crush the strike, demanded federal intervention.

Attorney-General Richard Olney, former lawyer for the railroads, was only too glad to act. He issued a blanket injunction against all strike activities. Although Debs felt that the strike could be won peacefully, violence broke out when the railroads hired thugs to be "deputy marshals" who beat up strikers, shot at demonstrators and set fire to freight cars. When Debs and other union leaders refused to yield to the injunction, President Cleveland sent several thousand federal troops to Chicago, despite the protest of Illinois Governor John P. Altgeld, who declared the move unconstitutional. Thousands of armed deputies, police and troops clashed with strikers and sympathizers. Thirty men and women were killed and many wounded.

A federal grand jury indicted Debs and other American Railway Union officials for conspiracy against the government. They were released on bail only to be arrested again a week later, charges with contempt of court and violation of the injunction. Clarence Darrow defended the strikers, but his case was defeated. The strike was broken and the American Railroad Union destroyed. Debs, a democrat, was converted to socialism during his six-month prison sentence.

The great Pullman strike was one of the most controversial labor issues in American history. Though it failed, the nation was exposed to the injustices of the paternalism of Pullman, the consequences of federal intervention in a labor dispute, and the complicity of the Attorney-General in destroying the American Railway Union. Public sympathy was with Debs, who argued that the government sided with capital rather than with the working people, and the real lawbreakers were the railroads and the Attorney General. Years afterwards, the debate continued. In reply to an article on the strike by ex-President Cleveland, Debs wrote: "President Cleveland says that we were put down because we had acted in violation of the Sherman Anti-Trust laws of 1890. Will he kindly state what other trusts were proceeded against and what capitalists were sentenced to prison during his administration?"

The Populists

I was once a tool of oppression/And as green as a sucker could be;
And monopolies banded together/To beat a poor bum like me.
The railroads and the party bosses/Together did sweetly agree;
And they thought that there would be little trouble/In working a hayseed like me.
But now I've roused up a little/And their greed and corruption I see;
And the ticket we vote next November/Will be made up of hayseeds like me.

—*A Hayseed Like Me*, Populist song

Business was tightly established, and labor had organizations. By the latter part of the 19th century farmers were the voiceless and unrepresented. The producers of America suffered from falling prices for their labors and foreclosures on their farms. Farmers no longer could depend on the government for help, and though isolated and rugged individualists, they struggled to organize for survival. The first nationwide farmers' organization was the Grange, or Patrons of Husbandry, formed after the Civil War, and by 1873 there were granges in almost every state with most of the strength and numbers in the Midwest. The granges broke the isolation of the farmer, stimulating interest in politics, culture and education.

In 1890 Congress passed the McKinley Tariff, the highest protective tariff to date, raising duties on manufactured goods and causing severe hardship on the farmer. The Farmer's Alliance, born out of this governmental injustice, grew and spread, publishing newspapers, educating farmers and starting co-operatives, urging self-reliance. Between 1890 and 1892 the Farmers Alliance developed into the Populist Party.

The Populists were mainly farmers, but remnants of the Knights of Labor, suffragists, socialists and reformers joined this colorful political party. They were fiery, energetic and zealous in promoting their ideas. Their leaders were natural orators and reached out to the common people; it was above all a grass-roots movement. Mary Ellen Lease expressed what people were feeling all along: "Wall Street owns the country. It is no longer a government of the people, by the people, for the people, but a government of Wall Street, by Wall Street, and for Wall Street. Our laws are the output of a system that clothes rascals in robes and honesty in rags." The Populists aimed to restore government to the "plain people and abolish the rule of privilege and monopoly."

In the 1890 elections the Populists sent twenty senators and representatives from the farmlands to the capitol. Their politics were winning the people, and in 1892 the newest party was after the presidency.

The Populists held their first national convention July 4, in Omaha, Nebraska, and drafted a dynamic and progressive platform, declaring their purposes to be at one with the Constitution. Pledging to work for equal rights and equal privileges "for all men and women of this country," the Populists laid out their program beginning with solidarity with the labor movement, government ownership of the railroads, and a new national currency, "a just, equitable, and efficient means of distribution to the people," free and unlimited coinage of silver and gold and a graduated income tax. The Populists demanded nationalization of telegraph and telephone services, land reform, the abolition of the Pinkerton system ("a menace to our liberties"), election reforms, and opposed any government aid to any private corporation. Progressive as they were in most areas, the Populists were a "down home" American party, believing as did conservatives in restrictive immigration. They regarded new immigrants as a threat to labor unions.

The Populists' candidate James B. Weaver won a million votes, but President Cleveland was re-elected. The panic that swept the country soon after closed factories and banks, and caused severe inflation. Farm prices collapsed. Farmers argued for coinage of free silver as a way of relieving the crisis, while conservatives believed that only the gold standard was stable. (To which the fiery prairie orator William Jennings Bryant replied at the '96 convention: "…you shall not crucify mankind upon a cross of gold.")

Populists flocked to the Democratic party to support Bryant, a Democrat from Nebraska who spoke the Populist language. The eastern Democrats and the former president opposed Bryant, giving strength to the Republicans. The campaign, starring Bryant, was spectacular. He toured throughout America, making up to ten speeches a day, appealing to laborers, farmers, progressives and liberals. It was a close race, and McKinley won by a half million votes. After the defeat of Bryant, the Populists as a political force faded, but their ideas were influential for many decades after.

Child Labor

Children rise at half-past four, commanded by the ogre scream of the factory whistle; they hurry, ill fed, unkempt, unwashed, half-dressed, to the walls which shut out the day, to dust and merciless maze of the machine. Here, penned in little narrow lanes, they look and leap and reach and tie among acres and acres of looms. Always the snow of the lint on their faces, always the thunder of machines in their ears. A scant half-hour of noon breaks the twelve-hour vigil, for it is nightfall when the long hours end and the children may return to the barracks they call "home," often too tired to wait for the cheerless meal which the mother, also working in the factory, must cook after her factory day is over. Frequently at noon and at night they fall asleep with the food unswallowed in the mouth. Frequently they snatch only a bite and curl up undressed on the bed, to gather strength for the same dull round tomorrow, and tomorrow, and tomorrow.

—Edwin Markham, Children in Bondage, 1914

Children had always been used as cheap, docile labor in America, but with industrialization, the horrors of child labor were out in the open. The 1900 census showed that there were two million children under 16 employed in the factories, fields and mines, and in the new age of reform the public began to be aware of the evils of child labor through writings and publicized investigations.

Industrialists resisted reforms, threatening to move their factories and business out of states that supported child labor laws. In many families the employment of children meant survival, and children of impoverished families desperately clung to their jobs. Proposed legislation affected only factory labor. In 1916 Congress passed a law forbidding the shipment in interstate commerce of the products of child labor, but this was considered unconstitutional. Congress later passed a law taxing products of child labor, but this too was ruled out by the Supreme Court.

Children as young as six worked night shifts in canneries. Youngsters made a few cents an hour on tobacco plantations and in factories manufacturing cigars and cigarettes. Seven year-olds picked cotton in sweltering fields. Breaker boys worked ten to twelve hours a day in mines picking out slate from coal. Children of migratory workers labored in fruit and vegetable fields as long as their parents. Many children worked at home, taking care of younger ones while their parents worked.

Children who worked in the factories, fields and mines suffered from ill health and accidents, and if they survived, grew up bent and sickly, illiterate and without hope. Children of seven were old enough to work at the glass factories, working in the heat of the ovens, inhaling the powdered glass, often suffering horrible burns from fragments of molten glass. In the Gulf States little children worked in the shrimp and oyster industries, little hands eaten by the acid of the shellfish. Mills ran two shifts, a day shift and a night shift, for maximum profit. Factories and sweatshops were poorly lit and children suffered several times more accidents than adults. The conditions of work for children were unsanitary and unsafe by any standards. States varied in their child labor laws, some had age limits of 12 or 14, but these laws were difficult to enforce.

Child laborers came from all races and many immigrant groups. The practice of employing children continued until the New Deal of the 1930s, which finally outlawed child labor. For many years afterward, however, in fields and factories, some employers continued to use children, in violation of the law.

This square was sewn by Lolly Font whose mother worked in the textile mills at the age of 12.

SERVANTS WANTED
Passage guaranteed
to new world
good wages....

Give me your huddled masses....
yearning to breathe free.

...We ho
evident th
that they
with certa
among th
pursuit of

" We hold these truths to
be self-evident: that all
men and women are created
equal..."

Seneca Falls
1848

1859

HARPERS FERRY

DRA

PULLMAN

STRIKE

Populist Movement 1892

CHILD
LABOR

NEWS

"COMMUNIST
CAUSE STR

"BREAD AND ROSES"
1912

LUDLOW

VOTE
YES
ON
WOMENS
SUFFRAGE

EQUAL SCHOOLING
SOUTH 1960s

VIETNAM VETERANS AGAINST THE WAR

WATTS 1965

Student Uprising 1970

Equal Education

The most deadly of all possible sins is the mutilation of as child's spirit.

—Erik Erikson

John Adams and Thomas Jefferson felt that self-government was impossible without the education of all Americans, rich or poor. In the 1830s new ideas of education from Europe promoted progressive change in schools and the way in which children were taught. Non-sectarian, tax-supported public schools began to be formed in many state and spread throughout the United States in the latter part of the 19th century.

Yet children of color were excluded from public schools, enslaved blacks were not allowed to read or write, and after they were freed, could only attend separate, unequal schools. Chinese and Japanese children were segregated into "oriental schools," and Mexican, Latino and Indian children were also denied equal education. Indian children on reservations were forced by missionaries to deny their own culture, language and customs. Children of poor families remained illiterate because they had to work from morning until night. Poverty-stricken children who did attend school often could not learn because they were hungry. Girls were often denied education, and women were excluded from college and many professional schools.

Wealthy families could afford nursery schools, prep schools, the best colleges and universities. "It's not what you know but who you know" were the words the powerful and elite establishment lived by. I.Q. tests were designed for the evaluation of, upper and middle class whites, and they were used to designate many minority children as "below average" and retarded, excluding them from further education.

Even when schools were integrated, ideas remained segregationist. The values taught in school were all WASP values, the heroes and historical events portraying the superiority of the white man and his culture. Still, children are taught that Columbus "discovered" America, that pioneers "won the West" and to remember the Alamo. Textbooks, teachers and administrators have perpetuated myths and stereotypes about minorities and women. Omission of the struggles and achievements of minorities and women have given us all a dangerously narrow view of our past, not to mention the damage done to the consciousness of all children.

In many states textbooks are being revised to include minorities; curriculum and teacher training are establishing a multicultural concept in education. Ethnic stories are not being taught in high schools and multicultural programs are used in the early grades. The process of changing centuries-old concepts is slow and difficult, and often tokenism and patronizing attitudes prevail.

Yet important changes are coming about. In the Lau vs. Nichols case of January 1974, the Supreme Court ruled that the San Francisco system discriminated against non-English speaking Chinese students by failing to help them overcome their language barrier, thus denying them a "meaningful opportunity to participate in the public education program." Because of this decision millions of non-English speaking children across the nation, Asians, Latinos, Mexican-Americans, can now learn in their native languages, participating in the first bilingual public education programs. The Lau vs. Nichols decision was the first time in U.S. history that the court recognized the needs of non-English speaking children.

Red Baiting in Union Strikes

In the fall of 1919 there were three large strikes, in all of which red baiting occurred and the real issues of the strikers were ignored. When Boston policemen struck over long hours, poor pay and bad working conditions and agitated to join the American Federation of Labor, they were accused of being "Bolshevistic" and subversive. *The Wall Street Journal* declared, "Boston in chaos reveals its sinister substance. Lenin and Trotsky are on their way." Newspapers inflamed the edgy public further with scare headlines and warnings of imminent Red takeovers. All the striking policemen were fired and a new police force was recruited.

When thousands of steel workers walked off the job, protesting low wages, deplorable conditions and long working hours, they faced the same accusations of being Bolshevistic. The government and the press emphasized the radicalism of the strikers and accused unions of "Bolshevizing" American industry. The strike became violent with many bloody confrontations between workers and police. In the face of a public hostile to labor and the powerful United States Steel Corporation, the strike failed.

Miners were angry that the coal industry had prospered during the war, but miners' wages stayed the same because of a wage agreement made in September 1917 to run for the duration of the war. When coal operators didn't raise wages after the war, miners agitated for a new wage contract. In November 1919 the United Mine Workers Convention, under the leadership of John L. Lewis, resolved to terminate the wartime contract and call a nationwide strike unless their demands were met and a new agreement signed. Coal operators refused to consider these demands.

Lewis declared a strike announcing, "The United Mine Workers of America are now embarking upon the greatest enterprise ever undertaken in the history of the trades union movement." He stated that the purpose of the strike was for the "right to a fair wage and proper working conditions," that "no other issue is involved and there must be no attempt on the part of another to inject into the strike any extraneous purposes."

It was inevitable that during a year when other strikers were being condemned for their radical and "Red" actions, miners on strike would be treated the same way. Conservatives and anti-labor people and mine owners demanded that the government prevent and "insurrection" led by communists. A chief spokesman for coal operators released to the press a statement that the coal strike was being undertaken on direct orders from Trotsky and Lenin and financially backed by Moscow. Other inflammatory propaganda was spread and widely publicized as evidence against the coal miners.

Federal Judge Anderson issued a temporary injunction to prevent the walkout. Lewis accused President Wilson and his cabinet of "sinister financial interests" and charged that the injunction was a curtailment of the rights of citizens.

394,000 leaderless miners left the mines, and the fact that such a huge walkout occurred in spite of the federal injunction convinced the press and public all the more that "Reds" were behind it all. The U.M.W. leaders were ordered to cancel the strike, and even after they did, the workers were reluctant to return to work. During that time the Fuel Administration had to conserve heat, factories were shut down, workdays cut, rail transportation limited. Attorney General Palmer, who saw Reds everywhere, was convinced that a Bolshevist revolution was around the corner.

In a final effort to end the strike Judge Anderson cited Lewis and 83 other U.M.W. officials for violation of the injunction. Meanwhile President Wilson authorized the Fuel Administration to offer the striking miners a flat 14 percent wage increase and promised that a commission would investigate their other grievances. In the face of these events, the solidarity of the remaining strikers was broken, and the President's plan was accepted. The workers got a 27 percent increase but no change in hours or working conditions.

Since that time the tactic of red baiting has reappeared time and time again in workers' strikes, in political protests and in struggles for civil rights.

The Molly McGuires

Men, if you must die with your boots on, die for your families, your homes, your country, but do not longer consent to die like rats in a trap for those who have no more interest in you that the pick you dig with.

—John Siney, head of the Workingmen's Benevolent Association,
after a mine explosion took the lives of 179 men, 1869

Between 1840 and 1870 over 20,000 Irishmen came to Schuylkill County in Pennsylvania's anthracite country. They left poverty in Ireland to find unspeakable hardship and frequent disaster in the coalfields of America. They became workhorses owned by the mine operators, laboring six days a week from dawn until dusk for eleven or twelve dollars a week. Men suffered from "miner's knees," black lung diseases, injuries, overwork and hunger. Mine owners refused to install emergency exits that could save miners' lives in an explosion, they did not install ventilating and pumping stations, and spared expenses by not installing sound scaffolding. Irish workers were considered expendable. Even children were used for separating slate from coal as it poured down the chutes, and boys as young as seven would work until exhaustion for one to three dollars a week.

The miners organized for the eight-hour day in 1868, forming the Workingmen's Benevolent Association of Schuylkill County. The strike failed but the organization remained, and miners continued to agitate for a big union.

Franklin Benjamin Gowan, head of a huge monopoly, the Philadelphia and Reading Railroad, was also president of the railroad's subsidy, the Philadelphia Coal and Iron Company. Ruthless and ambitious, he saw the organizing miners as a threat to his profits and control. In 1873 Gowan hired the Pinkerton Detective Agency to break the union, charging that the patriotic fraternal Irish organization, the Ancient Order of Hibernians, had a militant, terrorist caucus, the Molly McGuires.

James McParlan, a twenty-nine-year-old native of Ireland, was the Pinkerton spy sent to infiltrate the Order of Hibernians to entrap militant miners in a conspiracy against the mine workers. There never has been any evidence of the actual existence of the Molly McGuires. Most historians believe that the group was a fabrication Gowan used to brand the miners who organized as violent, dangerous men, providing an excuse to crush union activity.

Impatient for the Pinkerton spy to turn up evidence against the miners, Gowan decided to force a showdown. He announced a twenty percent pay cut. The miners went on strike January 1, 1875.

The mine operators, led by Gowan, launched a campaign of terror against striking miners. Several miners were killed by mine operators' vigilantes, and many were beaten and wounded. Several union leaders and the wife of a miner were murdered. Led by the Ancient Order of Hibernians, the mines fought back. Union leaders were arrested and charged with conspiracy.

The leaders imprisoned and many killed, the rank and file of the Ancient Order of Hibernians continued to resist. The press carried inflammatory stories inspired by Gowan of miners' violence and the terrorism of the Molly McGuires who were supposedly attempting to overthrow society by inspiring strikes. The strike took its toll on the families of the miners, and children began to die from hunger. Women, men and children would go into the woods to dig for roots and herbs to subsist. After six months of suffering, the miners were defeated by starvation. The union was beaten and organizers blacklisted, Miners were forced to accept the twenty percent pay cut.

But the miners continued to fight back. Gowan was determined to wipe out union activity once and for all. Militant miners were brought to trial, and the Pinkerton spy McParlan testified that the miners were Molly McGuires who murdered a patrolman. In a trial that was a mockery of justice, five miners, all of whom had been active in the 1875 strike, were found guilty. Other miners were convicted for other murders only on the testimony of McParlan. Between June 1877 and January 1879, nineteen miners were hanged. They were executed not for the accused crime, or even of being Molly McGuires, but for being union organizers fighting the cruel system of the coalfields and the men who ran it.

Coxey's Army

O say, can you see, by the dawn's early light,/That the grass plot so dear to the hearts of us all?
Is it green yet and fair, in the well-nurtured plight,/Unpolluted by Coxeyites' hated foot-fall?
Midst the yell of police, and the swish of clubs through the air,/We could hardly tell if our grass was still there.
But the green growing grass doth in triumph yet wave,/And the gallant police with their buttons of brass
Will sure make the Coxeyites keep off the grass.

—satiric song, 1894

Millions of Americans were unemployed in the Panic of 1893 as business collapsed, banks failed and industries went bankrupt. While farmers and workers and their families suffered, J.P. Morgan, Rockefeller and Carnegie expanded their holdings.

The government was besieged with demands for public relief. Thousands of unemployed roamed the country. There were demonstrations for federal assistance, but no action from the government. On Easter Sunday, 1894, Populist Jacob S. Coxey of Massilon, Ohio led five hundred unemployed people to Washington. The refrain of the Coxey's Army song was: "Hurrah! Hurrah! We want the jubilee!/ Hurrah! Harrah! Hard working men are we!/ We only want a chance to live in this of the free,/ Marching in the Coxey Army."

Coxey proposed that Congress authorize a public works program that would absorb America's unemployed, and marched on Washington to publicize his plan. This march, a living petition to President Cleveland, received widespread publicity. The ragged, impoverished band, arriving in Washington D.C. on May 1, symbolized the plight of millions, and made the well-to-do highly nervous. There were many other "armies of the unemployed," but Coxey's Army was the only one that made it to the Capitol. An army of police was waiting for them at the end of Pennsylvania Avenue. Coxey and other leaders were arrested for walking on the grass, and club-welding police dispersed the demonstrators.

Coxey, who had prepared a speech to be read from the steps of the Capitol, issued this statement:

Up these steps the lobbyist of trusts and corporations have passed unchallenged on their way to the Committee rooms, access to which we, the representatives of the toiling wealth producers, have been denied. We stand here today in behalf of millions of toilers whose prayers have not been responded to, and whose opportunities for honest, remunerative labor have been taken away for them by unjust legislation, which protects idlers, speculators and gamblers.

Wobblies

Workers of the world, awaken!/Break your chains, demand your rights.
All the wealth you make is taken/By exploiting parasites.
Shall you kneel in deep submission/From you cradles to your graves?
Is the height of your ambition/To be good and willing slaves?

— from a I.W.W. song by Joe Hill

The Industrial Workers of the World, "Wobblies," were founded in Chicago, 1905. They used music and humor to spread their cause, and their meetings and protests were enlivened by their own songs. Wobblies were called "bums" and worse, to which they answered in song, "Hallelujah, I'm a bum."

In the early years of the twentieth century unskilled workers were the most exploited class of people, unorganized and ignored by the American Federation of Labor and other trade unions. By the second decade of the twentieth century two percent of the population owned 60 percent of the nation's wealth, while nearly a half lived in poverty. Not only did the working class not receive their fair share of earnings, they did not receive their full rights as citizens.

The Wobblies dedicated themselves to changing all this. They fought for human rights over property rights. "Big Bill" Haywood, Wobbly leader, spoke of the hypocrisy of mine owners who could "wreck whole populations," then become maudlin over the destruction of a mill.

The I.W.W. gave hope to migrant workers, miners, cowboys, lumberjacks and the unemployed. Local I.W.W. halls become the refuge of the outcast and jobless. Songs and stories gave the downtrodden worker a sense of solidarity and purpose. "It makes no difference what your color, Creed, or sex or kin. If you are a worker, then its kick right in and join" goes one Wobbly recruiting song.

While the A.F. of L. under Samuel Gompers attacked "Asiatic coolie-ism," the I.W.W. welcomed Chinese and Japanese to its ranks. While other unions supported the world war, the I.W.W. came out against it, resolving, *We condemn all wars and for the prevention of such, we proclaim the anti-militarist propaganda in time of peace, thus promoting class solidarity among the workers of the entire world, and in time of war, the General Strike in all industries.* Once when a group of them were arrested, they were asked, "Who's your leader?" And they replied, "We all are."

Wobblies were at their peak of strength in 1912 at Lawrence, Massachusetts, a major center in a belt of textiles mills owned by the powerful American Woolen Company. On a cold January day mill workers began a spontaneous strike in response to a cut in already low wages. The Wobbly local in Lawrence called for help from fellow members, and they poured into the mill town, organizing soup kitchens and picket lines. "Big Bill" Haywood and Elizabeth Gurley Flynn, one of the first women union leaders, urged the workers to unite, to use direct action but no violence. Lawrence was a Massachusetts town of immigrants, and at least twenty-five nationalities were involved in the strike. United, they held out for nine weeks and won wage increases—a victory inspiring mill workers across the nation. During the Lawrence strike there was an attempt to frame the I.W.W. as saboteurs. Twenty-eight sticks of dynamite were planted in the town by a businessman who was on the school board. He was arrested, convicted, but was let off with a fine of $500. Two Wobblies and a Lawrence strike leader were arrested for the death of a women picketer who was killed by the militia, and held for five months without trial before they were acquitted.

Wobblies spoke the language of Thomas Paine and Jefferson, but they became scapegoats, labeled rabble-rousers and troublemakers. Because of their opposition to war, the War Department authorized the army to hunt them down and bring them in on charges of sedition and treason. The Wobblies became embroiled in defense trials, their energies and resources drained, and their leaders imprisoned.

The I.W.W. had many martyrs killed for their Wobbly beliefs and actions. Most famous is Joe Hill, convicted of murder in Utah and hanged, whose songs are part of folk vocabulary. ("Pie in the sky when you die" is from Joe Hill's "The Preacher and the Slave.") His last words were in a telegram to Bill Haywood: "Don't waste time in mourning. Organize." Frank Little, a half-Indian Wobbly, was lynched while organizing a strike of miners in Butte, Montana. Wobbly Wesley Everest was murdered by a lynch mob in Centralia, Washington, after a skirmish with the American Legion during an Armistice Day celebration. When a group of Wobblies arrived in boats at Everett, Washington in 1916 during a campaign for free speech, they were fired upon by vigilantes and policemen on the shore. Five workers died and scores of others were wounded.

The government soon began a post-war purge of radicals which led to new immigration and anti-alien laws. The Wobblies, though defeated, remained brave rebels to the end, leaving songs and legends that enrich American culture.

Sacco and Vanzetti

By systematic exploitation of the defendant's alien blood, their imperfect knowledge of English, their unpopular social views and their opposition to the war, the district attorney invoked against them a riot of political passion and patriotic sentiment; and the trial judge connived at—one had almost written cooperation in—the process.
— Felix Frankfurter, *The Case of Sacco and Vanzetti*

Nicola Sacco and Bartolomeo Vanzetti were young Italian immigrants accused of murdering a paymaster and his guard in a robbery of a shoe company in South Braintree, Massachusetts. Their case, because of its political nature, became an international issue during the 1920s.

Vanzetti was a laborer who worked at various jobs until he settled in Plymouth, Massachusetts. He led a factory strike and was blacklisted, where upon he became a fish peddler. He became a close friend of Sacco, a skilled worker in a shoe factory, who shared his idealism and political beliefs. Both men were active in organizing strikes, raising funds for the defense of labor leaders, leafleting and holding protest meetings. They were Italian anarchists opposed to capitalism and war at a time when the United States was swept by the Red Scare, which suspected all foreigners of subversion.

Sacco and Vanzetti were arrested on May 5, 1920, for the crimes of robbery and murder and found guilty. Although there was no concrete evidence against the men, the judge and jury were determined that they be convicted for their political beliefs.

Sacco and Vanzetti waited for six years in prison as the execution date was continually being postponed because of the fervor of public protest. Appeals were denied, and they were finally executed by electric chair on August 22, 1927. Sacco wrote in his last letter to his son:

But remember always Dante, in the play of happiness don't use all for yourself only…help the weak ones that cry for help, help the persecuted and the victim because they are your better friends; they are the comrades that fight and fall as your father and Bartolomeo fought and fell…for the conquest of the joy of freedom for all…

And Vanzetti had these words for himself and Sacco and America:

If it has not been for this thing I might have lived out my life among scorning men. I might have died unmarked, unknown, a failure. This is our career and our triumph. Never in our full life could we hope to do such work for tolerance, for justice, for man's understanding of man, as now we do by accident. Our words—our lives—our pains—nothing! The taking of our lives—the lives of a good shoemaker and a poor fish peddler—all! This last moment belongs to us—this last agony is our triumph.

Across the nation there were hundred of demonstrations protesting the execution of these two men. Rallies were held around the world decrying this American act of injustice and inhumanity, and petitions flooded the State Department. In New York 50,000 people gathered in Union Square and in small Italian vigils were held for Sacco and Vanzetti.

These two men were the scapegoats representing those in America who were aliens either in nationality or political belief. The country was to see a return of national hysteria in the McCarthy era of the 1950s with the trial and execution of Ethel and Julius Rosenberg.

Bread and Roses, 1912

"BREAD AND ROSES"
1912

Better to starve fighting them than to starve working!

—Lawrence strikers

More than half of the 30,000 strikers who successfully challenged the textile industry in Lawrence, Massachusetts, were women and children. No union instigated this strike. It was a spontaneous reaction to conditions of corporate-induced poverty.

A year earlier 146 women and girls died in the Triangle Shirtwaist fire in New York City. The workers were mostly young and from immigrant families, earning pitifully low wages. The doors of the factory were locked to keep out union organizers, and the women either suffocated in the smoke and flames or leaped to their deaths from the window onto the street.

At Lawrence the workers at mills owned by the American Woolen Company were poorly paid, and on the first payday of the year, January 11, 1912, the employers cut wages to insure the same huge profits to offset losses resulting from newly passed federal laws reducing the work hours of children under 18 and women from 56 to 64. Upon receiving their pay envelopes the workers shouted, "Short pay! Short pay!" They poured out of the factories into the streets in protest. Soon labor organizers and strike sympathizers came to Lawrence to help. When 15,000 workers who were demonstrating outside a mill were hosed with icy water in freezing temperatures, the strikers were further united and determined.

Women were involved both in the picketing and the resulting violence. Two pregnant women lost their babies as a result of beatings, nursing mothers were jailed, one was shot and killed. The winter was bitterly cold and food for the strikers was short despite the unceasing efforts of eleven I.W.W. soup kitchens and the Franco-Belgian cooperative bakery. The children, half-starved, had to be evacuated to the homes of strike supporters in New York. The first group of 150 children was escorted by Margaret Sanger and her assistants and greeted by a crowd of 5000 people at Grand Central Station. A week later, forty children headed for Philadelphia were separated from their parents at the Lawrence railway station by 200 policemen. Mothers were beaten and arrested on charges of "neglect and improper guardianship."

The brutality of authorities in trying to suppress a strike of hungry exploited workers shocked the country, and resulted in a Congressional investigation of the strike. The ensuing public reaction played a part in the textile corporation's eventual capitulation. On March 1, the American Woolen Company announced 7 ½ percent increases in 33 cities.

Historians of the labor movement feel that this strike was significant for its unfailing idealism. The workers were demanding a right to dignity, not just survival. The young mill girl's banner read: "We want bread and roses too."

—Sharron Carleton

Ludlow, 1914

I chose the Ludlow Massacre for my square long before Richard Nixon resigned and Gerald Ford became President and chose Mr. Nelson Rockefeller as his Vice President. But at the time I began to speculate about the possibilities of power in the hands of an unelected president and the new aura given the office of the Vice Presidency. It wasn't hard to guess that Mr. Ford would choose the former Governor of New York. I am from the East Coast, and as long as I can remember Rockefeller has been running for the Presidency of the United States. What does this have to do with Ludlow? Well, Ludlow is a little piece of the Rockefeller past, a lost history that never even crossed the minds of those Senate investigators. Too bad, because while we were carefully appraised of how much money this Rockefeller had (and wasn't it an awful lot of money?), we were never told how he got it. Of course everyone knows that he inherited it from his grandfather, the Great John D., who made his money by cornering every source of oil in the country and because of his ruthless methods was forced to throw dimes in the streets to buy a little affection back from those he had robbed.

But that was the grandfather, and over the years the dimes turned into philanthropic institutions softening the blows and dulling the memory.

Now back to 1914 Ludlow, Colorado, a small mining community in which the Colorado Fuel and Iron Company operated. This company was owned by one John D. Rockefeller, Jr., grandfather of our Vice President. The miners in this town formed a union, the United Mine Workers of America, and although conscious of the anti-unionism and power of the Rockefeller clan, they were forced by economy necessity to call a strike. Since the town was owned by the company, the miners were quickly evicted from their homes and forced to live in tents on the outskirts of town. The strike dragged on, and the company, determined to keep the mines in operation, called out the National Guard. Vigilantes and the National Guardsmen frequently took pot shots at the women and children in the campground when the men were on the picket lines. To protect their children the miners dug a cave inside the larger tent, where one pregnant woman and thirteen children were instructed to hide in case of danger. On the evening of April 20, 1914, the miners' tents were covered with oil and lit. When they ran to escape the fire, the National Guardsmen opened fire with machine guns. The women and thirteen children died of suffocation in the fire. Another women and five miners were gunned to death. Many were wounded. Later, John D. Rockefeller commented that is was a principled battle to protect working people from unionism. When indignant reporters pressed Rockefeller on the issue, he responded that he was above all a Christian….I suppose that's a rich man's way of celebrating Easter.

I grew up in New Jersey and have been studying Rockefeller history for some time. I'm not surprised that they have as much money as they have. Rockefeller history is in practically every state in this country and in the world. Wherever you find oil and mineral resources, you will find a Rockefeller. Did the Rockefeller Commission deal fairly and honestly in its investigation of the C.I.A.? Perhaps it was another "principled battle," the kind of honesty of Ludlow, the kind of fairness that caused a guilty conscience to throw dimes in the streets of the ghetto.

—Marge Murphy

The Palmer Raids

In the 1920s no organized groups protested the alien's loss of civil rights. Deportation cases were striking the friendless and the poor, the isolated and the ignorant. Radicals who might have objected were left alone. The figures showing that only 15 percent of the aliens arrested could raise bail or obtain counsel are indicative of their sorry condition and of their inability to resist. Of those ordered deported, only 2 percent sought release on habeas corpus, and five-sixths of these failed.

—William Preston, Jr., *Aliens and Dissenters*

In post-World War America, anti-German feeling expanded into anti-foreign sentiment, and distress over the Bolshevik revolution of 1917 in Russia wrought repression upon aliens and dissenters, as well as many who were neither.

Attorney-General A. Mitchell Palmer, launching a crusade to save America from the "Red Menace," succeeded in fanning the flames of national anti-communist hysteria. In November of 1919, as an exercise for bigger things to come, the Bureau of Investigation agents under the directive of Palmer raided the offices of the Union of Russian Workers and 300 people were arrested. J. Edgar Hoover, zealous head of the General Intelligence Division of the Bureau, or the alien radical division, urged that either excessively high or no bail at all be set for people captured in these "inquiry dragnets," and that they be held in isolation without the interference of defense lawyers. The Bureau had developed a system for dealing with radicals: arrest and deportation. The 1918 Immigration Act gave the Secretary of Labor the power to deport any alien thought to be an anarchist or revolutionary.

On January 2, 1920, the Palmer Raids swept through 70 American cities, resulting in the arrest of 10,000 people. The target of the raids were members of socialist and communist organizations, but agents rounded up people in bowling alleys, cafes, homes and public meetings. In Massachusetts 39 bakers who had gathered for the purpose of establishing a co-op bakery were hauled into jail. Some people were arrested on the streets because they "looked radical." Said Palmer of the victims of his raids, "Out of the sly and crafty eyes of many of them leap cupidity cruelty, insanity and crime; from their lopsided faces, sloping brows, and misshapen features may be recognized the unmistakable criminal type." After they had been given the third-degree, kept for days in crowded cells, the haggard prisoners were photographed for the newspapers so the public could see what dangerous "wild-eyed Bolsheviks" looked like.

In Boston 4000 people taken from the immigration station for transfer to Deer Island in the harbor were forced to march in chains to the dock. Held in deplorable, crowded conditions at Deer Island, one prisoner went insane, two others died of pneumonia, and one killed himself by jumping out the window.

Eventually over half of the 10,000 arrested were released without charges but only after suffering terror, imprisonment and abuse at the hands of authorities. The rest were confined for long periods of time, and hundreds of men and women were deported. Many aliens did not know their rights and were easy victims; others were tortured or intimidated into being members of radical organizations.

Palmer and Hoover were not concerned with warrants or due process or any legalities in the raids. Neither were the press or the majority of the public, who were caught up in the climate of fear and hysteria. Congress, for the most part, approved of Palmer's handling of the so-called "dangerous" elements in American society, and six months after the raids, an immigration law was passed which punished aliens for simply possessing literature showing sympathy for radical doctrines.

A dozen lawyers drew up a report, Illegal Practices of the Department of Justice, declaring that the Palmer Raids had trampled the Constitution and violated the First, Fourth, Fifth and Eight Amendments. The report accused the government of lawlessness, of using agent provocateurs, third-degree tortures, illegal searches, seizures and arrests.

The Palmer Raids succeeded in suppressing dissent, spreading fear, curtailing union activities, and fostering a tradition in America of anti-foreign, anti-dissenter sentiment. The mission of hunting for radicals, broadened the role and powers of the Bureau and it would ultimately become the formidable F.B.I., which has continued its activities of domestic surveillance and creating paranoia in America.

The Women's Vote

Yes, your honor, I have many things to say; for in your ordered verdict of guilty, you have trampled under foot every vital principle of our government. My natural rights, my civil rights, my political rights, my judicial rights, are all alike ignored. Robbed of the fundamental privilege of citizenship, I am degraded from the status of a citizen to that of a subject; and not only myself individually, but all of my sex, are, by your honor's verdict, doomed to political subjection under this, so-called, form of government.

—Susan B. Anthony, when charged with voting illegally in the presidential election of November 1872

The judge in this case wished he had never asked if she had anything to say on her behalf. She persisted in arguing for her cause, concluding, "I shall never pay a dollar of your unjust penalty." The former abolitionist Ms. Anthony and many other eloquent, courageous and tireless suffragists argued, wrote, rallied, leafleted, marched, picketed and were imprisoned in the cause of women's vote.

The territory of Wyoming granted the vote for women in 1869 and by 1898 three new states, Colorado, Utah and Idaho had followed suit. By 1914 eleven states had extended voting rights to women, but the suffrage movement had yet to have an impact on Congress. When Susan B. Anthony presented a petition with 20,000 signatures to Washington on the women's vote, she was rebuffed by the reply that the petition was worthless because it was signed by "only women."

There were two large suffragist groups, the Congressional Union, which later became the National Women's Party, a militant group led by Alice Paul, and the National Women's Suffrage Association headed by Anna Howard Shaw and Carrie Chapman Catt who opposed radical tactics. The former group organized a parade of 5000 women down Pennsylvania Avenue in 1917 and the marchers had to be protected from outraged mobs by the National Guard. The movement in England and the militancy of the suffragists there gave impetus and examples to American women. Sylvia Pankhurst came to American, emphasizing the oppressed workingwomen's need for the vote and equal pay. Her mother Emmeline and sister Christobel also came to give encouragement, emphasizing the role of militancy in winning the vote.

When the National Council of Women met in Nashville, Tennessee in 1897, the *Nashville American* newspaper published the hackneyed putdown of the suffragists:

Whether they will accomplish their ultimate purpose and establish women on an absolute equality with man we have very serious doubts. We believe that natural laws will settle these questions…and we have an idea that no mater how far women may go in their projects of equality with men, that sooner or later they will retract their steps and finally will come to the place where the laws of nature and nature's God intended them.

Women out for votes suffered ridicule from editors, cartoonists, clergy, jeering crowds and other women. They were heckled and stoned, their banners and placards torn, their offices ransacked. Some women went on hunger strikes in jail and had to be force-fed. They marched down Fifth Avenue in New York, held vigils in Washington, and had meetings and more meetings. In the South, racist propaganda declared that the suffragists advocated intermarriage. An anti-suffragist piece read: "Women in suffrage states are serving on juries in murder cases, commercialized vice cases, and whiskey cases. Do you like the prospect for your wife and daughters? If not, WAKE UP AND DEFEAT WOMAN SUFFRAGE."

Women activists retaliated with their own literature and often responded with humorous, satiric verse and writings. This was a reply to those who charged that the vote would "unsex" women:

It doesn't unsex her to toil in a factory
Minding the looms from dawn until night;
To deal with a schoolful of children refractory
Doesn't unsex her in anyone's sight;
Work in a store where her back aches unhumanly–
Doesn't unsex her at all you will note,
But think how exceedingly rough and unwomanly
Woman would be if she happened to vote.

Women argued that naturalized immigrant men were allowed the vote, freed male slaves were given the vote, and that by denying women the vote, they were classified with "idiots, lunatics and criminals." On February 10, 1919, sixty-five members of the National Women's Party burned President Wilson in effigy, protesting his lack of support for the federal suffrage amendment. The women were arrested and imprisoned. Some suffragists looked upon the vote as the end goal of their cause, but pioneers such as Alice Paul, Jane Addams, Matilda Joslyn Gage, Crystal Eastman and Susan B. Anthony (who did not live to see women vote), were dedicated to continuing progressive political change.

By the summer of 1920, thirty-five states had passed the Nineteenth Amendment in their legislatures, and the approval of only one more state was needed to make it a part of the Constitution. In August of that year, the state of Tennessee ratified the Susan B. Anthony Amendment, and it became the law of the land. Carrie Chapman Catt said, "That vote has been costly. Prize it!"

Lynching

Nor is the South responsible for this burning shame…The sin against the Negro is both sectional and national; and until the voice of the North shall be heard in emphatic condemnation and withering reproach against these continued ruthless mob law murders, it will remain equally involved with the South in this common crime.
— Frederick Douglass, 1892

Whenever the Constitution comes between me and the virtue of the white women of South Carolina, I say to hell with the Constitution!
—Senator Cole Blease on lynching, 1930

The specter of lynching, violent death at the hands of a hysterical, bloodthirsty white mob has always haunted black people in America. The Ku Klux Klan, formed during Reconstruction by white supremacists, terrorized blacks in the South with its threatening, flaming crosses in the night, its beatings and killings. White mobs without hoods and sheets dealt out punishment to blacks who got "uppity" or stepped out of line. Lynchings not only went unpunished, but were often condoned and even actively supported by politicians and law enforcement officers.

Between 1889–1921 there were 3467 recorded lynchings. By the turn of the century black people had launched an active campaign against mob terror. Black Congressman George H. White of North Carolina introduced in 1900 the first bill aimed at making lynching a federal offense. Ida B. Wells, a black woman, published the first statistical pamphlet on lynching, "The Red Record;" she was run out of Memphis and her Free Speech Newspaper offices were destroyed by whites for exposing the facts behind the lynching of three young blacks.

On July 28, 1917, 10,000 black men, women and children marched down Fifth Avenue in New York in the Silent Protest Parade organized by the National Association for the Advancement of Colored People. Some marchers bore banners reading, "Mr. President, Why Not Make America Safe for Democracy," and "Thou Shalt Not Kill."

In 1922 the NAACP rallied support for the Dyer Anti-Lynching Bill with a *New York Times* ad which asked this shocking question: "Do you know that the United States is the Only Land on Earth Where Human Beings are Burned at the Stake?"

Six black soldiers returning from fighting in the World War in Europe were among the 28 blacks burned at the stake between 1918–1921. During the "Red Summer" of 1919 twenty-five separate major race riots took place at various cities including Chicago, Omaha, East St. Louis and Washington which resulted in the deaths of hundreds of black people.

A report of 1933 by the Southern Commission on the Study of Lynching found apologists for lynching from every walk of life—doctors, teachers, judges, preachers—who like the lynchers themselves felt that blacks were inferior and whites were justified in using any means to "keep the Negro in his place." Most lynchings in the thirties were of blacks falsely accused of raping white women or insulting whites. Some victims were not accused of any crime at all.

Blacks have not been the only victims of lynchings. People considered "foreign" have been lynch victims as well as "outside agitators" and other people of color. In Los Angeles in 1871, 21 Chinese, including women and children, were lynched, some of them hung from the city's lampposts. The possibility of this kind of mob violence remains as long as there are racial tensions in the United States. In October 1974, in south Boston, a black man passing through a crowd of whites protesting school bussing was beaten and would have been lynched had he not been rescued by a gun-welding patrolman.

The Flint Strike, 1937

When we walked out on you,
We set you back on your heels,
Goody goody!
So you lost some money and now
You know how it feels.
Goody goody!

—parody of pop song sung by Flint workers

Strikers had everything to lose during the Great Depression. In 1930 auto workers who staged a strike were defeated and blacklisted. But the continuing bad working conditions and low pay made auto workers increasingly angry and determined to improve their situation. They were an exploited labor force, sometimes paid as low as 20 cents an hour, made to do monotonous work at a speeded-up pace without any relief. Spies within the plants reported on union activities, and anyone suspected of organizing was fired and sometimes beaten. During the heat wave in the summer of 1936 men were worked to exhaustion, and there were many deaths on the assembly line at the General Motor plants.

On November 18, 1936, there was a sit-down strike in the G.M. plant in Atlanta, the next month at the plant in Kansas City, then in Cleveland, then Anderson, Indiana, and Norwood, Ohio. The most critical strike that was to change the course of union history was at Flint, Michigan, the heart of the G.M. empire, January 4, 1937. Union sympathizers came by the thousands from all over the Midwest, fearing that the Flint strikers would be killed by G.M. vigilantes. Giant picket lines formed around the three occupied plants at Flint, thousands of women and children gathering to protect their husbands, fathers, and sons. Children marched in the cold with signs saying, "We're behind our Dads," and "Give Us a Chance for Better Food and a Better Life." Pickets and strikers stood firm, day and night in the bitter cold. Women brought food to the men in the plants and hoisted their little children to the windows to see their fathers and boost their spirits.

The nation watched for news of this huge strike at Flint, which soon became a symbol for working people everywhere, as the workers continued to hold out day after day, week after week. The three plants were well organized into stalwart communities, the men sleeping in half-completed cars, writing, playing cards and growing stubby beards.

Sitting down in the plants was a new tactic and looked upon with horror by the industrialists who saw the occupation of private property as criminal and communistic. The "giants of industry" could not understand that these thousands of men occupying the plants had earned their share of G.M. by their blood and sweat. As to be expected, red-baiting was used as a tactic of the management to discredit the auto workers. Alfred P. Sloan, refusing to recognize the United Auto Workers Union, accused the strikers of trying to "Sovietize" the industry as a "dress rehearsal for Sovietizing the entire country." He advocated using troops to eject the strikers by force. John L. Lewis, head of the C.I.O. retaliated by charging that the country's largest corporation was breaking the law by violating the Wagner Labor Act.

An injunction was issued for the eviction of the strikers, and the Flint workers responded by calling out from the plants: "Damn the injunction, damn the courts, damn the army and double damn General Motors!" Though unarmed, they vowed they would fight to the last man to defend themselves if force was used against them.

After G.M. tried unsuccessfully to freeze the men out, they decided to starve them out. Police came with tear gas when the women arrived with food for the men. The women had to fight the tear gas and the police, and inside the men used water hoses on the police and tear gas bombs. As one women said later, "Nothing was going to stop us getting food to our men." The pickets threw stones, coal, and bottles at the police and stood their ground. A woman addressed the mammoth picket line from the union sound wagon: "We don't want any violence; we don't want any trouble. We are going to do everything we can to keep from trouble, but we are going to protect our husbands."

As the state police and troops mobilized, women prepared themselves, inspiring solidarity by returning to the picket line after being gassed. Thousands joined the Women's Auxiliary, and the Women's Emergency Brigade armed themselves with 2 by 4s.

The Governor of Michigan, Frank Murphy had the order for troops of the National Guard to clear the plants, but fearing he would be held responsible for a bloodbath, could not issue it. On the morning of the 44th day of the strike, General Motors surrendered, announcing they would recognize the union and negotiate with the strikers on their grievances. In the plants the sit-downers, many disbelieving the announcement, found themselves surrounded by a massive wildly cheering crowd. They marched out of the factories that had been their home for so many weeks in a jubilant two-mile parade: chants of "freedom, freedom" and "join the union" could be heard over the honking of horns and singing.

The haggard forces of strikers and women and children of Flint had won over the nation's largest industry. Within a year wages had increased substantially and conditions improved. The Flint victory inspired the nation's working people, and soon other downtrodden, exploited workers would organize their own sit-down strikes and win.

The Bonus Marchers, 1932

The United States Army turned on to American citizens—just fellows like myself, down on their luck, dispirited, hopeless. My mood was one of despair. It was an experience that stands apart from all others in my life. So all the misery and suffering had finally come to this—soldiers marching with their guns against American citizens. I had nothing but bitter feelings toward Herbert Hoover that night.

— Thomas L. Stokes, reporter who witnessed the Bonus March

The Depression was a miserable, devastating period for Americans. Perhaps those who felt it most bitterly were the unemployed veterans of World War I who had fought to "save the world for democracy" and faced joblessness and starvation at home. In 1924 Congress had passed a bonus bill for veterans which provided adjusted service certificates for every ex-servicemen, payable in twenty years. To the hard-hit veteran, relief was desperately needed during the Depression, and early in 1932, Representative Wright Patman of Texas introduced a bill providing for immediate payment of the bonus.

Unemployed veterans of World War I came from all over the United States to rally support for the bill in Washington, D.C. The "Bonus Expeditionary Force" was a cross section of different races, different backgrounds, from cities and towns all over the country. Beginning in May of 1932 thousands of veterans journeyed to Washington, hopping freights, hitching rides, walking. Some brought their families with them, piled into old jalopies and trucks. All had no means of employment or support; they were destitute, hoping for government actions and the passage of the new bonus bill. Veterans and their families found housing in abandoned tenements, or made shelters out of cardboard boxes, scraps of tarpaper roofing and anything they could salvage, borrow or beg. Up to twenty-five thousand marchers came to Washington, a poor people's lobby at the great capitol. But the Senate voted against the Patman bill by a huge margin of 62 to 18.

Yet the veterans, more hopeless than ever, did not leave Washington, much to the chagrin of the Hoover Administration. More members arrived and the Bonus Army continued to parade around the capitol. They had nowhere else to go.

Hoover was determined to evict the Bonus marchers. The police evacuated the hungry, shabby veterans and their families from buildings and tents. Some fighting ensued, and Hoover ordered the War Department to send in the army to help the police.

General Douglas MacArthur was the commander of the forces: four troops of cavalry, four companies of infantry, a machine gun squadron and six tanks. His aide was Colonel Dwight D. Eisenhower, and another officer was Major George S. Patton, Jr. Troops using tear gas cleared the old buildings and set them on fire. Then MacArthur sent his forces across Anacostia bridge where the marchers were encamped on the mud flats along the river. Thousands of men, women and children fled before the charging troops. There was no resistance possible as troops lobbed tear gar bombs into the huts and set them on fire. Jalopies were wrecked, veterans' possessions were destroyed. Many marchers were injured by clubs, bayonets, sabers and thousands were stricken by gas. An eleven-week-old baby died from being gassed, and a child was partially blinded. Two veterans were shot to death.

The victorious MacArthur said, after veterans were driven out by gas, tanks and guns, "This was a bad-looking mob. It was animated by the essence of revolution." The public, however, was outraged by the brutal action of the government, siding with the plight of the destitute marchers, the veterans and their families, beaten from the capitol by their own troops. After this incident the American people were ready for a new administration. The president became the butt of every Depression joke. "Hooverville" was the name of any town of unemployed people and "Hoover blankets" were newspapers used by the poor to keep warm. The protest was registered at the polls in November as Roosevelt and the New Deal were the people's overwhelming choice.

The San Francisco General Strike, 1934

Longshoremen were hired off the streets "like a bunch of sheep" said Harry Bridges, union leader, describing the "shape up," a mob of workmen struggling for only one day's work, desperately hoping for the foreman's favor. Every morning at 6 a.m. the San Francisco Embarcadero was like a slave market. Longshoremen were unorganized, the only union being the corrupt "Blue Book," a company union. With the Depression, the misery of longshoremen's lives deepened. The tonnage of all Pacific coasts ports had fallen off, and more and more workers competed for fewer jobs on the waterfront. Longshoremen demanded that the shipping magnates negotiate in collective bargaining. They refused and fired four leaders of the union. On May 9, 1934, 12,000 longshoremen went out on strike in all Pacific coast ports, and by May 23, eight maritime unions and 35,000 workers walked out on the job.

The Industrial Association, the employer's organization and the San Francisco Chamber of Commerce refused to negotiate and accused the strikers of un-American radicalism. The demands of the longshoremen were for a dollar an hour wages, a six hour day, a thirty-four hour week and a union hiring hall, but the Industrial Association responded only by red-baiting. The *Chronicle* ran a story entitled "Red Army Marching on the City," and other West Coast papers also played up the "communist threat" theme.

Led by employers, the police were determined to smash the picket lines by force. Only July 3, carloads of police with gas and riot guns fought with the striking longshoremen using bricks and clubs in a furious bloody battle. The violence continued on July 5, known as "Bloody Thursday." Police clubbed hundreds of longshoremen and passersby and wrecked the union headquarters of the longshoreman. The governor then sent in two thousand armed National Guardsmen. "We cannot stand up against police, machine guns and National Guard bayonets," said Harry Bridges, who didn't mean they were surrendering either.

The brutality used to put down the strikers shocked the public. The solemn funeral of two workers shot by police made a huge impression and contributed to bringing on the general strike. Thirty thousand marchers slowly walked down Market Street behind the coffins. The demonstration of a huge mass of men and women united in their grievances and resentment galvanized the working people of the city.

Union locals met and voted for a general strike, calling for solidarity of workers. On the morning of July 16, San Francisco was paralyzed. Stores were closed, streetcars did not run, factories were empty, machines were still. Nothing moved except for giant picket lines. Several thousand additional National Guardsmen were called to the city and mobs of vigilantes destroyed union offices, wrecking progressive newspaper offices and the longshoremen's soup kitchen. Police arrested several hundred elderly men on charges of communist conspiracy.

On July 19, conservative A.F. of L. officials announced that the central labor body had voted to end the general strike. But the workers returned to their jobs knowing their strength, unity and power. By October the longshoremen had won what they had asked for in wages and hours. They had gained a hiring hall, a method for democratic rotary hiring to replace the cruel "shape up." The strike had won dignity for workers— it was a great moral victory.

America's Concentration Camps

Snow upon the rooftop
Snow upon the coal;
Winter in Wyoming—
Winter in my soul

Miyuki Aoyama
Heart Mountain, Wyoming,
An American Concentration Camp

By now, the snowball was big enough to wipe out the rising sun. The big rising sun would take a little more time, but the little rising sun which was the Japanese in countless Japanese communities in the coastal states of Washington, Oregon and California presented no problem. The whisking and transportation of Japanese and the construction of camps with barbed wire and ominous towers supporting fully armed soldiers in places like Idaho and Wyoming and Arizona, places which even Hollywood scorned for background, had become skills which demanded the utmost of America's great organizing ability.

—from the preface to *No-No Boy*, by John Okada

They were farmers, workers, owners of small businesses, artists, teachers, either American-born or well-settled immigrants, when suddenly by Presidential edict, they and their families were forced out of their homes, rounded up and sent to relocation camps where they were confined for three years.

Many Japanese Americans still remember well the hysteria after the bombing of Pearl Harbor, and the sudden contempt for everything Japanese. They remember the evacuation announcements giving them a few days' notice to sell their property and possessions and prepare to report to the "reception centers," bringing only what they could carry. Many can recall the deplorable conditions of the camps, the depressing barracks they had to live in, the poor quality of food, and the constant surveillance.

America expected a full invasion of the country, with Japanese Americans acting as a fifth column, performing acts of sabotage, although no basis for this fear was ever found. Executive Order 9066, signed February 19, 1942, by President Roosevelt, authorized the evacuation, and the public welcomed the move. Over 110,000 men, women and children of Japanese ancestry, two-thirds of whom were American citizens by birth, were sent to ten camps: Manzanar and Tule Lake in California, Granada in Colorado, Topaz in Utah, Heart Mountain in Wyoming, Minidoka in Idaho, Poston and Gila River in Arizona, Rohwer and Jerome in Arkansas.

Prior to this ultimate in "yellow peril" hysteria, Japanese had endured over fifty years of racism and discriminatory immigration and civil laws. Like the Chinese they were not allowed to be naturalized as American citizens; they were excluded from trade unions, deprived of equal protection of the law and socially segregated. In 1908 Theodore Roosevelt negotiated the "Gentlemen's Agreement" with Japan whereby Japanese immigrants in America would be accorded improved treatment if Japan would limit emigration. In 1913 the Alien Land Law prohibited any Japanese from owning property, and in 1924 Congress passed a law prohibiting aliens "ineligible for citizenship", clearly aimed at Japanese, from entering the country.

The first generation, the Issei, went into agricultural work in large numbers, filling the need for labor and before the 1924 Immigration Law, sent for "picture brides" and raised families. Japanese men and women worked in agriculture in Hawaii, California, Oregon and Washington and other regions.

They developed farming techniques and advanced agricultural industries. Many petitioned repeatedly for naturalization in vain but kept struggling to gain equal rights. They wanted to set down roots, and they found they could buy land in their American-born children's names.

For all those of Japanese ancestry in the desolate camps during World War II, everything they had worked for was lost. Greedy buyers had taken advantage of their plight and bought their goods for only a fraction of what they were worth. Much of their property and possessions was stolen from them outright. In the camps the traditional family unit was destroyed. Children saw the spirits of their parents crushed. No one could take pride in their work or activities. They were internees, each one a ward of the government: they were American prisoners of war in America.

Some resisted, as in the Manzanar riot in which two Nisei were killed by guards and many wounded. A few brave individuals challenged the constitutionality of Executive Order 9066 in court and lost. Over 25,000 young Japanese Americans served in the armed forces, many distinguishing themselves by extraordinary bravery, and imprisoned parents received notices of the deaths of their sons in Italy and France and held memorial services on the barren grounds of the camps.

This quilt square was stitched by Jeanette Arakawa, who spent three years of her youth in the relocation camp of Rohwer. She comments:

The coal referred to in the poem by Miyuki Aoyama are the piles which could be found at certain locations in the camps. Coal was used for cooking in the mess halls as well as for burning in the pot-belly stoves in each room or living unit. The temperature in Heart Mountain plunged as far as thirty below zero.

Japanese were released from the camps in January 1945, and were encouraged to "scatter." Some did make new lives in cities in the Midwest and East, but many wanted to return to their farms and businesses on the West Coast. They all had to start their lives all over again.

Dedicated to preventing reoccurrence of such persecution, the Japanese American Citizens League launched a campaign to defend the rights of Asians in the United States. In 1953 Japanese were finally given the right of naturalization, and as a result of the efforts of Japanese Americans, Title II of the Internal Security Act (the Emergency Detention Act) was finally repealed, September 14, 1971.

Desegregation of Schools in the South

Tessie was the first Negro child to step into that white school. There were three of them, 'the three little niggers' they were called, but Tessie stepped into the building first. I saw it with my own eyes, and I won't forget it, you can be sure. That night I said my prayers, just as I have for over sixty years, but I added something. I said, "Lord, you have started giving New Orleans your attention, at last. The whites are screaming at Tessie and me, but that's because they know You are watching; and they're mad, because they know they're bad, and they'll soon be punished soon now that You've decided

to take a hand in our lives here." That's what I said, and some more, too—because I had to repeat myself, I was so happy. The way I see it, Tessie and I can be cursed every day, and it will only mean we're nearer our freedom.

—grandmother of a six-year-old black child who integrated a New Orleans school, 1960, quoted from *Children of Crisis* by Robert Coles

It's more for America than for me.
—James Meredith, first black student to enroll at the University of Mississippi

Jim Crow laws of the 1890s, practices in the South aimed to separate black people from white, deprived the Negro of the right to vote and established segregation in schools, housing, employment, transportation and public places. It was South's answer to the Northern-imposed agenda of the Reconstruction and a re-establishment of white control and supremacy.

The landmark Supreme Court decision, Brown vs. Board of Education would be a turning point in American history, launching the Civil Rights movement. In an unanimous decision May 17, 1954, the Supreme Court declared racial segregation in public schools unconstitutional. The Court declared. "Separate educational facilities are inherently unequal…Liberty under law exceeds to the full range of conduct which an individual is free to pursue, and it cannot be restricted except for a proper governmental objective. Segregation in public education is not reasonably related to any proper governmental objective."

A precedent was set and therefore segregation in every sector was unconstitutional. Acts of courage of the first to challenge a segregated restaurant or business or park inspired others to action. Sit-ins and boycotts sprung up throughout the South. Black people were integrating lunch counters, polling booths, and public transportation. Black and white civil rights volunteers—Freedom Riders—risked their lives and limbs to register voters in the south. Rosa Parks refused to give up her seat at the front of the bus and went to jail. Martin Luther King, Jr., organized thousands of people into a massive non-violent boycott that forced desegregation of business in Montgomery, Alabama.

In 1955 integration of Northern schools began, but in the South there was violent resistance. Desegregation was part of the unfinished business of Reconstruction, but to the South, it was always seen as an abomination to be resisted and a violation of states' rights. Governors of some states threatened to abolish public schools rather than permit black and white children to sit in the same classrooms, and in some areas schools closed down rather than integrate. In Little Rock, Arkansas, 1957 Governor Faubus called out the Arkansas National Guard to block the entry of nine black teenagers to the Central High School. The 101st Airborne Division of the U.S. Army as well as federalized troops in Arkansas had to be mobilized to escort the black students to school amidst the furious white mobs.

In the aftermath of federally enforced integration black people continued to be terrorized by violence and brutality. Black homes and businesses were bombed, blacks were beaten and lynched. Whites who favored integration were intimidated and suffered economic reprisals. In Birmingham, Alabama, in 1963 a Baptist church was bombed, killing four young black girls. But the white segregationist who kept saying "never!" did not overcome.

Now in Southern cities and towns where ugly scenes of racism made the headlines in the late fifties and early sixties, black and white children are peacefully attending the same schools. The principal of Central High in Little Rock is Morris Holmes who is black. Yet the struggle continues and is not confined to the South. A violent out-pouring of racism spewed in south Boston, 1974 in the ugly familiar scene of angry racist crowds in an uproar over busing. Of busing to achieve integration, Pam Storay, a black student at Parkview High School in Little Rock, says, "I get to know more students than before, whites and blacks, and even a few Indians and Chinese. Those Boston students should try it."

There were great heros who dedicated their lives to the cause of integration in the South. This quilt square celebrates the very youngest who broke the barriers and awakened a nation's conscience. Little black children resolutely faced the dangers of being the first to integrate elementary schools, suffering the pain of loneliness, of being teased by white children and threatened by adult racial supremacists. Miriam Nixon, who is white, sewed this square. It was the sight of these brave little Americans walking to school with heads held high through shouting mobs held back by armed soldiers that inspired her to find out more about this kind of courage and endurance, and started her familiarity and friendship with black people.

Vietnam Veterans Against the War

I am American.
I am American dying in Asia.

—William J. Simons, from a poem, "My Country" Winning Hearts and Minds;
War Poems by Vietnam Veterans

The hundred years ago a young pamphleteer described colonialists who left the revolutionary army during the bitter winter at Valley Forge as "summer soldiers and sunshine patriots." Recalling the images of Tom Paine, Vietnam Veterans saw themselves as "winter soldiers."

Throughout the decade of protest against the war in Indochina, many activist organizations tried to arouse the conscience of the nation, recalling the principles of the Declaration of Independence, the Constitution and the ideals upon which our country was founded. No other group more dramatically evoked the spirit of the first American revolution than a large organization of veterans who had fought in Indochina and returned, some wounded and disabled for life, determined to tell the truth about the war to the American people.

These young men were drafted or joined the armed forces were sent to Vietnam by their country to defend America, defeat the communism and save people from totalitarianism. They found themselves betrayed and part of an occupation army rather than a liberating one. Many found themselves more sympathetic to the ideals of the National Liberation Front than the South Vietnamese government they were sent to support.

Veterans returned bitter about their experiences and the senselessness of the death of their comrades. Many returned to find themselves jobless, with few veteran benefits and some languished in substandard veterans' hospitals suffering from wounds and effects of "agent orange". Guilt for participating in the genocidal policy of the war moved many veterans to commit themselves to ending it.

By the end of 1970 the United States, finding its Armed Forces demoralized and often mutinous, changed its tactics and began to "Vietnamize" the war, funding the South Vietnamese army and using massive U.S. air support of "saturation" bombing. During this most destructive phase of the war, the veterans held the "Winter Soldier Investigation" hearings in Detroit where 600 veterans testified to U.S. atrocities in Vietnam.

Thousands of Vietnam Veterans marched along the historic Revolutionary War Route from Morristown, New Jersey, to Valley Forge, Pennsylvania. In the spring of '71 they demonstrated in the Capitol, using guerilla theater to bring the war home, calling their encampment, "Dewey Canyon III—a limited Incursion in the Country of Congress." In a symbolic act of their rejection of the war and policies of the government, 800 men threw down the medals and campaign ribbons they had been awarded in Vietnam at the steps of the Capitol. A former Marine Sergeant from Connecticut, Jack Smith expressed the feelings of many veterans:

We now strip ourselves of the medals of courage and heroism…these citations for gallantry and exemplary service…We cast these away as symbols of shame, dishonor and inhumanity. Our tale is one of a Vietnamese people whose hearts were broken, not won. Our commanders were not concerned with lives, but body counts. Our testimony gives definition to words like genocide, racism and atrocity.

Vietnam Veterans Against the War organized self-help groups to rehabilitate those who returned plagued by drug addiction, alcoholism and psychiatric problems. The organization also agitated for better veteran benefits. In a government move to destroy VVAW, members of the organization, the Gainesville 8, were indicted for "conspiracy" during the Republican convention on '72. An F.B.I. informant within the membership testified against those on trial. After 14 months of persecution, the veterans were finally acquitted.

Watts

There's new strategy coming in. It'll be Molotov cocktails this month, hand grenades next month and something else next month. It'll be ballots, or it'll be bullets. It'll be liberty, or it will be death.

—Malcolm X, 1964

At the famous March on Washington, August 1963, Martin Luther King gave his stirring "I have a dream" speech at the foot of the Lincoln Memorial to a crowd of 250,000 people. The following year three civil rights workers were murdered in Mississippi, a series of riots broke out in eastern ghettos protesting murders of blacks. Alabama state troopers attacked people marching from Selma to Montgomery. There were other incidents of assassinations and beatings of black people and white sympathizers.

Langston Hughes once asked in a poem, *What happens to a dream deferred? Does it dry up like a raisin in the sun? Or does it fester like a sore? Or does it explode?*

The answer came from a community near Los Angeles name Watts, in the summer of 1965. It was a year when the hopes of blacks were rising, with the catalyst of Vietnam and civil rights agitation. There was new assertiveness among blacks and rising anger towards the continuing neglect, benign and otherwise, by the government. The life in Watts was like that in many black ghettos; there was high unemployment, poor housing, constant police surveillance and harassment. Watts was ready to explode.

Marquette Frye and his mother were driving home one evening and were stopped 100 yards from their home by a patrol car. The police asked them to get out of the car and wanted Frye to show them his driver's license. One policeman shoved his mother aside. Frye shoved back. He was arrested. The next day the community reacted—it was the accumulation of pent-up anger from thousands of such incidents. The people were tired of being shoved around, and they rioted against life in the ghetto, burning stores and their homes and looted. The National Guard was called and the shooting began. Thirty-five black people were killed. Two policemen were shot by other policemen. Eight hundred and eighty-three people were injured and 3,598 arrested. Property losses exceeded $46,000,000. Portions of Watts were burned to the ground. East 103rd Street, the heart of Watts, was known as Charcoal Alley.

Hattie Kelly sewed the Watts square. She was living just two blocks away from the spot where the holocaust began. Hattie and other black women of the quilting group felt that "Watts was more than just a riot." Most of the blacks in this country saw it as a strong outcry against injustice and oppression that had been accepted for too long. The outburst of anger from Watts gave blacks a certain sense of pride, and forced whites to face the reality of ghettos in America and of rising black protest. Soon after Watts there many "long, hot summers"—in Newark, New York, Chicago, Cleveland and Washington, D.C.

Watts of '65 had violence, but hope. Ten years later the scene there is peace yet despair. The federal money and liberal politics did not get to the root of the problems of Watts. Poverty programs, issued as appeasement to pacify the people, soon faded out. Though the government welfare system has instituted surface stability, unemployment is still the chief problem of the people of Watts, blacks continually get harassed and shot at by the police, and the dream is still deferred. The United States spent more money for a week of war in Vietnam than ten years in Watts.

The Student Movement

The overriding rule which I want to affirm is that our foreign policy must always be an extension of our domestic policy. Our safest guide to what we do abroad is always what we do at home.

—President Lyndon B. Johnson

We thought, and I say this with some embarrassment for my naiveté, that adults really mean what they said, that when Presidents speak of peace they don't mean war, that when terms like democracy are bandied about they don't mean totalitarianism of the center.

—Jesse Kornbluth, *Notes from the New Underground*

Did it all begin with the Civil Rights struggle, or with the 1964 Free Speech Movement at Berkeley or when hundreds of students in the spring of 1960 were washed down the marble steps of San Francisco City Hall at the hearings of the House of Un-American Activities?

All institutions were targeted: the university which Mario Savio labeled a great big "factory," the armed forces which David Harris told young men to "resist," the American system which Carl Ogelsby accused of being a "corporate state" and middle-class values which young people called hypocritical. And Dr. Benjamin Spock who raised them during the complacent Cold War years got arrested with thousands of his children in the biggest bust in U.S. history, May Day 1971.

The Vietnam War was the catalyst. On April 17, 1965, there was a march on Washington to end the war in Vietnam, organized by Students for a Democratic Society. In the spring of 1966 General Lewis Hershey announced that students whose academic standing was poor would be drafted. Faculty and students protested the use of grades for Selective Service purposes and many institutions refused to give the Selective Service any information. Students tried to stop troops trains, army buses, and blocked induction centers, risking arrests and beatings. Young men burned their draft cards while others went into exile in Canada.

Students demonstrated at laboratories that did military research, trashed ROTC buildings and blocked military recruiters and defense contractors from entering the placement centers. Students and faculty pointed out the "Vietnams" in our own country, the ghettos outside the privileged campuses, the destruction of the environment, the racism and poverty. In 1968 at San Francisco State College minority students organized the Third World Strike, demanding a comprehensive ethnic studies program, minority student and faculty recruitment, a responsive administration, and in the words of one picket sign, *"Education, not Regimentation."*

College teach-ins involved not only students and professors, but housewives, workers, everyone in the community, speaking their minds. Some students practiced civil disobedience; others leafleted and organized guerrilla theater. Students influenced LBJ's decision not to run again in '68. They boosted the campaigns of Eugene McCarthy and Robert Kennedy, and four years later, George McGovern. While most worked within the system, some felt it essential to cause disruptions ("No business as usual!" "Bring the

war home!"). There were bombings and acts of arson. The extensive surveillance of student groups and the infiltration of paid provocateurs and F.B.I. agents encouraged and often initiated violence.

Commencements became protests, students given awards by groups such as the D.A.R. and American Legion refused to accept them. Establishment speakers found they were welcome only at armed forces academies. Students invaded trustee meetings, formal dinners and ceremonies.

"The connection between the violence here and abroad must be made: the violence at home will not end while the violence abroad continues," warned Yale class speaker William M Thompson '69 at the graduation ceremony. "As long as the fighting continues at its present level, our opposition to the war will also continue. Immediate action must be taken to extricate us from the disaster that is Vietnam. The war must end now; and the fight for our cities, for our nation, for our people must begin."

In the spring of 1970, the U.S. invaded Cambodia. At Princeton, the bastion of collegian elitism, nearly half the student body came to the university chapel within an hour of Nixon's "incursion" speech to call for action. On May 4 at Kent State, Ohio, the heartland of Middle America, the National Guard was mobilized to put down student agitation. Governor James Rhodes called the protesters "worse than Brown shirts and Communists and vigilantes—they're the worse type of people that we harbor in America." Nixon called them "bums." From a grassy hill troopers fired on students walking to class. Four students were killed, ten wounded. A week later two students were shot to death and twelve others wounded at Jackson State, Mississippi, a predominantly black college.

With the withdrawal of U.S. troops and the reliance on air power and on the South Vietnamese Army, anti-war protest waned. Students who continued to agitate suffered expulsions for their part in campus disturbances, and some colleges accepted more apolitical students to cool the campuses. By 1975 when the war ended, the campuses were quiet.

The war in Vietnam lasted three college generations, each making a difference. Students ended the draft. They prevented the U.S. from waging total war on the Vietnamese people.

The square on the quilt was inspired by Allison Krause, one of the four students killed at Kent State. She had placed a flower in the rifle of a National Guardsman saying, "Flowers are better than bullets."

Farah Strike

It was people like Willie Farah who long ago stole our land and paid cheaply for our ancestors. It is time that we, the Chicanos, stand up and say that's enough.

—Farah striker

In May 1972 four thousand Chicano workers, eighty-five percent women, walked out on the job at Farah Manufacturing Company in Texas and New Mexico. Willie Farah, owner of the wealthy garment company, ran his operations on paternalism—air-conditioned plants, free donuts and bus rides up to work, but no job security, no maternity benefits, low pay, speed up and discrimination on the job. When workers tried to organize in 1969, Willie Farah refused to negotiate, firing union supporters.

The center of the strike was El Paso, Texas where the Farah Company had been growing rich off the labor of Chicano workers for over fifty years. The average take-home pay was $69 a week. When workers had a union rally, supervisors for Farah were taking pictures and writing down names of workers. When seven union supporters were fired the next day, hundreds of workers walked out. In the following weeks thousands joined the strike at other plants.

One young woman, Virgie Delgado and her three sisters worked in Farah to support their family of nine. As for so many other working women, it was a hard decision for her to walk out on the job, but she felt it was the only right thing to do and she called on others workers to strike as well.

My legs were shaking the whole time. We were really scared because we didn't know what was going to happen. My three sisters joined us and all these guys and girls followed us. By the time we got to the front door I looked back and saw 150 people behind us.

We were about to walk out the door when the supervisor stepped in front of me and asked us where did we think we were going. So I told him he had better step out of the way or I wouldn't be responsible for what I would do. Then he said for us to punch out and I said no,

we're walking out and he'd better get out of the way. He was really shocked that I talked like that so he moved out of the way and we walked outside. Then we saw all the other people outside who had left the day before and we were really happy. We started hugging each other and singing even though we didn't know each other. It was really something.

The strike involved nine plants, and the management of Farah, the biggest pants manufacturing company in the U.S., claimed that there was no strike, just an "unauthorized walkout." Farah obtained a court injunction that ruled pickets had to be 50 feet apart. Over 800 strikers were arrested. "If anything," said Willie Farah, "we've been guilty of keeping some people around here too long, hoping they would straighten out. The union did us a favor by cleaning house, getting the troublemakers out. With that fifth gone, the plant is more cohesive." He brought in busloads of Mexican workers from across the border to break the strike, pitting one group of exploited people against another.

Across the nation there were Support Farah Strikers demonstrations and "Boycott Farah" became a rallying cry. Supporters organized pickets of stores that sold Farah pants, and Farah Strike Support Committees were organized throughout the United States. Shoppers saw the picket lines, read the leaflets and refused to buy Farah goods.

In February 1974 Willie Farah, responding to heavy loss and pressure from the National Labor Relations Board, finally gave in and negotiated with strikers. He agreed to rehire fired strikers and to grant workers the benefits they were asking for. A union was born out of a victory for Chicano workers and became an example to working women everywhere.

The United Farm Workers

We are the Campesinos of the rich soil of this land; we are the poorest poor, the forgotten, whose destiny has been controlled by the lucky few who have plenty. Our lot was tossed about by law-makers, and then cast aside for final burial deep in the archives of Congress. We are Campesinos who bring food to the American table three times a day. In the fields we work from sunrise till sunset, under the hot sun of summer, in the freezing cold of winter for slave wages in order to survive...to feed and clothe our children. We are the Campesinos who were pitted one race against another, storing hatred in our hearts instead of understanding for each other. We were exploited, fired and replaced on the spot, and discriminated against by the few greedy.

— from the U.F.W. leaflet

The Campesinos, or field hands, were the most isolated of all of American's workers, away from public view, their attempt to organize beaten down with intimidation and brutality. Early strikers were costly in worker's lives, limbs and jobs. Not until 1965 when a farm worker's union was organized by Cesar Chavez, Dolores Huerta and others did a farm workers' movement really begin.

At an AFL-CIO convention in San Francisco, Walter Reuther of the United Auto Workers told the handful of farm workers' representatives, "When we first began, we were fewer than you. We were only seven." He said General Motors told the workers in 1935 the company could not afford to pay unionized workers, that they would go broke. Reuther pointed out, now the growers are saying the same thing to farm workers, The farm workers would receive further encouragement along with national publicity from Robert F. Kennedy, who came to Delano when Chavez was ending his 25-day fast in March of 1968.

The United Farm Workers' struggle became a movement in which everyone could help out: the shopper who looked at the "specially priced" grapes at the supermarket and pushed the cart on, the student who demanded the college serve only U.F.W. lettuce, the wine lovers who shopped only from a list of union approved wineries, and singers and performers who donated their talents to benefit concerts. Nuns, priests, students, children, teachers, men and women from all walks of life joined picket lines and demonstrations, boycotting stores that sold non-union produce. The boycott of California table grapes which began in New York City in 1968 proved effective in forcing growers to negotiate with the U.F.W.

U.F.W. victories have been won nonviolently, with patience and appeal to the conscience of the opposition. The movement is a "bread and roses" fight. Chavez, whose family was so poor he had to work in the fields instead of going to high school, has given the United Farm Workers a philosophy and purpose beyond willing better wages and conditions.

In 1969 he wrote a letter to E. L. Barr, President of the California Grape and Tree Fruit League in reply to the accusation that the U.F.W. uses violence and terrorist tactics, saying of the farm workers:

They have been under the gun, they have been kicked and beaten and herded by dogs, they have been cursed and ridiculed, they have been stripped and chained and jailed, they have been sprayed with poisons used in the vineyards. They have been taught not to lie down and die or flee in shame, but to resist not with retaliation in kind but to overcome with love and compassion, with ingenuity and creativity, with hard work and longer hours, with stamina and patient tenacity, with truth and public appeal, with friends and allies, with mobility and discipline, with politics and law, and with prayer and fasting. There were not trained in a month or even a year; after all, this new harvest season will mark out fourth full year of strike and even now we continue to plan and prepare for the years to come. Time accomplishes for the poor what money does for the rich.

Philip Vera Cruz who came in 1926 from the Philippines and is now second vice-president of U.F.W. recalls the conditions of work in his first farm labor job. "There were no decent toilet facilities and the sanitation was terrible. There were two drinking cups for thirty workers," and "workers got sick from diseases." He and other Filipino workers organized a strike of asparagus workers in 1948. Exploited Chinese and Japanese workers also organized their own separate groups. Strikes of one racial group could not succeed in building a union, he realized, and only the United Farm Workers by appealing to workers of all races could affect change. While Chicanos and Mexican immigrants make up the largest group in the U.F.W. and then Filipinos, and there are Arabs, Portuguese, blacks and whites in the U.F.W.

Agribusiness is an eight million dollar a year business in California where one fourth of all fruit and vegetables eaten in America are grown. The big companies earn immense profits from non-union workers. Poor workers often bring their families in the fields to help out, and children as young as eight pick fruit, in violation of child labor laws. Pesticides, sprayed from low-flying airplanes on plants and people alike are the chief cause of illness of the farm workers—the other is heat prostration.

The struggle of farm workers to be "free and human," in Chavez's words, is succeeding. Sanitary conditions in the fields have improved. The short hoe which has bent the backs of thousands of workers has been finally outlawed. In the summer of 1975 the United Farm Workers won a major victory when the California Agricultural Labor Relations Act was passed. It meant for the first time that farm workers were free to choose their own union.

The Ecology Movement

…If it is unpatriotic to tear down the flag [which is the symbol of the country], why isn't it more unpatriotic to desecrate the country itself—to pollute, despoil and ravage the air, land and water? Such environmental degradation makes the "pursuit of happiness" ragged indeed. Why isn't it unpatriotic to engage in colossal waste that characterizes so many defense contracts?

—Ralph Nader

This was a vastly beautiful land when the Indians lived in it, so full of natural wonders and breathtaking landscapes, clear waters, lovely fields and woods and bountiful resources. Now much of that magnificence is ruined. Americans have been using the country's resources as if they will last forever. Mountains, lakes, rivers, bays and forests have been devoured by "progress." Our coastlines have been marred by "development." The Great Lakes, rivers such as the Potomac and the Hudson are all polluted. So many combustible pollutants have been dumped into the Cuyahoga River in Cleveland that it is now inflammable. Lake Erie, once a beautiful and productive inland water, is now a dead sea. The air we breathe is sometimes so filthy and noxious that it endangers our health and is fatal to those with pulmonary illnesses.

Warning against people's destruction of the environment and consequent self-destruction have been issued by conservationists in the past, but during the sixties there arose a nationwide awareness of America's wasteful way of life, the severity of pollution and the lateness of the time. "Ecology" became the new household word for a movement which encompassed everything from recycling cans and bottles to stopping off-shore drilling and strip mining. Rachel Carson brought national attention to the dangers of pesticides to wildlife and humans in her bestseller, *Silent Spring*. A number of ecology organizations sprang up and some older ones such as the Sierra Club attracted a new following. Communities organized recycling centers and many youth groups launched ecology projects. People were made aware of everyday wasting of all forms of energy. When informed that automobiles caused 60 percent of air pollution, more people began to drive less and walk or bicycle short distances.

Speakers and programs throughout the country emphasized the immediate need for conserving energy and other resources. The United States—with only six percent of the world's population—consumes 40–60 percent of the world's resources. We waste billions of dollars of food and materials every year while many around the world starve to death. Producers dump milk to keep prices up while ghetto children go hungry.

Few of America's technological and scientific developments have been directed towards preserving or restoring what we have taken from nature. In his essay "Nature Under Attack," Barry Commoner writes:

The crisis in the environment reveals a potentially fatal flaw in the use of modern science and technology. We have developed an enormous competence to intervene in the natural world: we can release fearful nuclear explosions, spray insecticides over the countryside, and produce millions of automobiles. But at the same time we are unable to predict the full biological consequences of nuclear war or to avoid risks to our livelihood and health from the side effects of insecticides or from the smog that our autos produce. In the eager search for the benefits of modern science and technology, we have blundered into the accompanying hazards before we are aware of them.

Solutions to improve the environment are possible but industries refuse to comply because their foremost concern is maximum profit. Workers fearing loss of jobs are played off against environmentalists. If a town decides to pass a law preventing an industry from dumping in the local river, the company can threaten to move elsewhere, causing economic hardship to the people employed.

The ecology movement has called our attention to the destructive nature of our present lifestyle. Although this effort has influenced the thinking of Americans, a major reorientation of the government's priorities and resources is imperative. Environmentalists have agitated and lobbied for nationwide anti-pollution laws to be strictly enforced on industrial polluters. The federal budget provides token support for conservation of energy and resources, while major portions are allocated to defense industries. Industrial polluters not only go unpunished, they are given governmental assistance.

Conservationists' long-held concern about the eventual exhaustion of our fossil fuels has been ignored by government policy, and motorists' dependence on gasoline and the panic caused by the oil shortage has given oil companies greater advantages and record profits. No concerned effort has been made in seeking alternative sources of energy. The push to build nuclear plants proceeds helter-skelter with no known safe method of disposing of plutonium waste products that may endanger future generations. Many billion-dollar military projects have been mothballed after construction. The disposal of radioactive wastes has never been satisfactorily resolved.

America's proprieties must be clean air, water, effective public transportation, clean cities free of poverty. Our nation can abolish unemployment by embarking on an extensive program of reconversion of polluting and destructive industries into life-supporting systems. To avert environmental disaster and the resulting devastation to people, we cannot do otherwise. We have sent men to the moon, but here is where we live.

The Prison Movement

….we do not want to rule, we only want to live. But if any of you gentlemen own dogs…you are treating them better than we are treated here.
—an Attica inmate to observers, September, 1971

…prison can make you look back on a lifetime of bitterness…
—from a poem by Erika Huggins, Niantic Prison, 1970

Famous political activists, clergy, teachers and journalists have served time. Imprisonment for some was hardly a time of defeat. The socialist labor leader Eugene Debs was nominated for President in 1920, and while a prisoner in the Atlanta Penitentiary, he received nearly a million votes. Suffragettes wrote first-hand reports on prison condition that shocked the public and led to investigations. In Danbury Prison 1943, 19 conscientious objectors went on work strike to stop Jim Crow seating in the dining hall and after 135 days ended segregation in the prison.

In the last decade huge numbers of Americans were arrested in the cause of civil rights and peace, and experienced the horrors of prison for the first time. College students serving short sentences for blocking induction centers would walk out of jails full of people who would be going in and out of "the joint" for the rest of their lives. Contact with the poor and uneducated, and people of color who could not afford legal counsel deeply affected those who had "allowed" themselves to be arrested. They saw how women prisoners are given tranquilizers to keep them docile. Many were subject to abuse and sexual attacks by guards. By agitating for better conditions by fasting, petitioning and work strikes, prisoners suffered reprisals. "Troublemakers," those resisting the deplorable prison system, suffer longer sentences, and parole is used as a tool of control.

Prisoners protested "strip cells," poor food and recreational controls. In 1968, 500 prisoners in San Quentin went on work strike over their lack of legal rights when facing the Adult Authority. In 1970 an uprising at Rikers Island, New York City lasted for four days and 1500 prisoners were involved. 2100 prisoners were put into lockup for a work strike at Folsom Prison. Among their demands were abolition of indeterminate sentence and the Adult Authority, and the freeing of political prisoners. In 1971 inmates held two sheriffs' deputies hostage in a New Orleans jail for eight hours. Women prisoners in the New Orleans' Women Detention Home staged a sympathy strike.

The life of George Jackson exemplifies the injustice of the American penal system. When Jackson was 18 years old he was sentenced from one year to life for stealing $70 from a gas station, and most of his 11 years in prison were spent in solitary confinement. Time after time Jackson was denied parole, and in 1970 he was charged with killing a prison guard. On August 21, 1971, Jackson was transferred form Soledad to San Quentin where he was gunned down by a guard.

Shortly after George Jackson's death, an uprising at Attica Correctional Facility in New York State captured the nation's attention. On September 9, prisoners took 38 guards hostage and demanded better conditions. Governor of New York, Nelson Rockefeller, refused to come to Attica to help negotiations saying. "I do not feel that my physical presence on the site can contribute to a peaceful settlement." On September 13, state troopers, the police and National Guard surrounded Attica. Helicopters dropped tear gas and troops poured gunfire into the prison yard. During the siege there were reports that the inmates had brutally slain eleven guards but investigations showed all had died from gunfire. Some hostages testified that the prisoners had actually protected them with their bodies.

Forty-three citizens of New York State died at Attica Correctional Facility between September 9 and 13, 1971. Thirty-nine were killed and more than 80 were wounded by gunfire during the fifteen minutes it took the State Police to retake the prison on September 13. With the exception of Indian massacres in the late nineteenth century the State Police assault which ended the four-day prison uprising was the bloodiest one-day encounter between Americans since the Civil War.

—Officer Report of the New York State Special Committee on Attica

Tom Wicker, an observer at Attica during the siege wrote in an article "The Men in D Yard" (*Esquire*, March 1975):

In a country were so many wealthy or well-represented lawbreakers could go free, where the killers at Kent State and Jackson State had not even been prosecuted, where minorities—black and Mexican—American, for two good examples—suffered from openly prejudiced law in whole regions, where the poor and disadvantaged of all races usually felt the full weight of police, courts and prisons—in that country "the equal application of the law" was to be upheld in the case of the Attica brothers!

This square was sewn by Andrea Holman Burt, a young woman who is imprisoned in San Bernadino on a conspiracy charge. Andrea was active in the anti-war movement. She wanted this square to express the need for changing the prison system, showing hands from the outside reaching out to those behind bars.

Women Hold Up Half the Sky

In 1776 Abigail Adams warned her husband, "If particular care and attention are not paid to the ladies, we are determined to foment a rebellion and will not hold ourselves bound to obey any laws in which we have no voice or representation in governing this nation."

Two hundred years later, Abigail's words still resound. Since the mid-sixties, women have fought on many fronts. They had waited too long, supporting other movements, relegated to making the coffee and taking notes. The battle cry became "free our sisters, free ourselves." Women agitated for equal pay, equal hiring practices, set up women's centers, health clinics, childcare centers, galleries and presses. They fought against sexism in the media and in textbooks, opposed beauty contests, fought for birth control and abortion rights, and organized against rape and pornography. They challenged sexist laws and practices of various states, such as credit unions' discrimination toward women and a married woman's unequal right to property.

Consciousness-raising groups have brought women together for mutual support. Third World women have organized their own groups. With the lowest median income in America, women of color have fought for increased opportunities, exposed exploitation, and opposed racist standards of beauty and behavior.

Achievements of women in sports—the tennis and track stars, gymnasts and swimmers—have all enhanced the self-esteem of girls and women. Girls have joined the previously all-boys Little League, soccer and other sports. Title IV of the 1972 Education Amendments Act, through the efforts of Representative Edith Green, has won rights for women in education and has led the drive for women's athletic rights in schools. College budgets for men's sports are 30 times larger than the allocations for women's, and women have called attention to this gross inequality.

Women have struggled with little help from the federal government.

This administration has done nothing of significance in the field of women's rights, responsibilities and opportunities. Not a single important policy decision or legislative recommendations advancing women's rights has been made. Not only have fewer women been appointed to responsible positions than in past administrations, but the number of existing women office holders replaced by men in the present administration has reduced the net record to minus one. (Representative Constance Dwyer to President Nixon in 1969)

President Ford appointed John Paul Stevens to replace Supreme Court Justice William W. Douglas, ignoring pleas to appoint a woman in the all-male court.

The National Organization for Women (NOW) in 1967 demanded "the U.S. Congress immediately pass the Equal Rights Amendment to the Constitution to provide that 'Equality of rights under the law shall not be denied or abridged by the United States or by any State on account of sex.'" Needing five more states to ratify before adoption, The E.R.A. still continues to face opposition, and those against it have fostered erroneous fears it will ruin the institution of the family, create unisex toilets, draft women, etc. The E.R.A. will guarantee equality before the law for women, which the Constitution has yet to provide. In November of 1975, state equal rights were defeated in both New Jersey and New York.

In Mexico City during International Women's Year 1975 American women joined women from many countries to discuss common problems of struggling against patriarchal societies and to seek solutions. History or "herstory" has shown women the struggle has been continual. As feminist Robin Morgan says, "There's so much documentation now, so much awareness of the previous waves of feminism, of past female culture that is now being unearthed, I don't see it getting buried again." Women have found their cultural heritage, which has given them pride and inspiration for the battles ahead.

Men as well as some women view the women's movement as a threat. "What do you want, anyway?" is the perpetual question. Protest over the firing of Professor Marlene Dixon at the University of Chicago in February 1969 prompted this statement by Chicago Women's Liberation that says it all:

What does women's freedom mean? It means freedom of determination, self-enrichment, the freedom to live one's own life, set one's own goals, the freedom to rejoice in one's own accomplishments. It means the freedom to be one's own person in an integrated life of work, love, play, motherhood: the freedoms, rights and privileges of first class citizenship, of equality in relationships of love and work; the right to choose to make decisions or not to; The right to full self-realization and to full participation in the life of the world. That is the freedom we seek in women's liberation.

To achieve these rights we must struggle as all other oppressed groups must struggle; one only has the rights one fights for. We must come together, understand the common problem, despair, anger, the roots and processes of our oppression; and then together, win our rights to a creative and human life.

Bibliography

Abrams, Richard M., ed. *Issues of the Populist and Progressive Eras, 1892–1912*, Harper and Row, 1969.

Adler, Mortimer, ed. *The Negro in America*, Vol. 2, Encyclopedia Britannica, 1969.

Boyer, Richard O. and Morais, Herbert M., *Labor's Untold Story*, United Electrical, Radio and Machine Workers of America, New York, 1955.

Bernstein, Irving, *The Lean Years*, Houghton Mifflin, 1960.

Bernstein, Irving, *The Turbulent Years: A History of the American Worker, 1933–1941*, Houghton Mifflin, 1970.

Brown, Dee, *Bury My Heart at Wounded Knee*, Bantam, 1971.

Catton, Bruce, *Never Call Retreat*, Doubleday, 1961.

Common Sense, Newspaper of the Peoples' Bicentennial Commission, Washington, D.C.

Conrat, Maisie and Richard, *Executive Order 9066*, California Historical Society, 1972.

Deloria, Vine, Jr., *Behind the Trail of Broken Treaties*, Delta, 1974.

Deloria, Vine, Jr., *We Talk, You Listen*, Delta, 1970.

Filler, Louis, *The Crusade Against Slavery 1830–1860*, Harper and Row, 1960.

Fischel, Leslie A., Jr., Quarles, Benjamin, *The Negro American: A Documentary History*, William Morrow, 1967.

Fiske, John, *The Critical Period of American History 1733–1789*, Houghton Mifflin, 1888.

Foner, Eric, *America's Black Past*, Harper & Row, 1970.

Franklin, Bruce, *From the Movement Toward Revolution*, Van Nostrand Reinhold, 1971.

Franklin, John Hope, *From Slavery to Freedom*, Vintage, 1969.

Fusco, Paul and Horowitz, George D., *La Causa: The California Grape Strike*, MacMillan, 1970.

Goldberg, Art, "Vietnam Vets: The Anti-War Army," *Ramparts*, July, 1971.

Harney, Thomas R. and Disch, Robert, ed., *The Dying Generations: Perspectives on the Environmental Crisis*, Dell, 1971.

Hofstadter, Richard, Miller, William and Daniel, Aaron, *The United States, the History of a Republic*, Second ed., Prentice-Hall,1967.

Hughes, Langston and Melzer, Milton, *A Pictorial History of the Negro in America*, Crown, revised ed. 1968.

Jackson, George, *Soledad Brother*, Bantam, 1970.

Jacobs, Paul and Landau, Saul, *To Serve the Devil, Vol. I: Natives and Slaves*, Random House, 1971.

Labaree, Benjamin Woods, *The Boston Tea Party*, Oxford University Press, 1964.

Leinwand, Gerald, *Air and Water Pollution*, Washington Square Press, 1969.

Martin, Wendy, ed., *The American Sisterhood: Writings of the Feminist Movement, from Colonial Times to the Present*, Harper and Row, 1972.

Markham, Edwin, Lindsey, Benjamin B., Creel, George, *Children in Bondage*, Heart's International Library Co., 1914.

Matthiessen, Peter, *Sal Si Puedes: Cesar Chavez and the New American Revolution*, Random House, 1969.

Morgan, Robin, ed. *Sisterhood is Powerful*, Random House, 1980.

Murray, Robert K, *Red Scare: a Study in National Hysteria, 1919–1920*, University of Minnesota Press, 1955.

Nee, Victor and Brett, Yu, Connie Young and Wong, Shawn Hsu, eds., *Special Issue: Asian America, Bulletin of Concerned Asian Scholars*, Vol. 4, No. 3, Fall, 1972.

Preston, William, Jr. *Aliens and Dissenters*, Harper & Row, 1963.

Raper, Arthur F., *The Tragedy of Lynching*, Dover, 1970.

Rennie, Susan, Grimstad, Kirsten, *The New Women's Survival Sourcebook*, Alfred A. Knopf, 1975.

Renshaw, Patrick, *The Wobblies: The Story of Syndicalism in the United States*, Doubleday, 1967.

Rosen, David M., *Protest Songs in America*, Aware Press, 1972.

San Francisco Bay Area Farah Strike Support Committee, *Chicanos Strike At Farah*, United Front Press, 1974.

Seeger, Pete, *The Compleat Folksinger*, Simon & Schuster, 1972.

Skolnik, Jerome H. *The Politics of Protest*, Ballantine Books, 1969.

Taylor, A. Elizabeth, *The Woman Suffrage Movement in Tennessee*, Bookman Associates, 1957.

Vera Cruz, Philip A., on the United Farm Workers Union, conversations with Connie Young Yu November 9 and 10, 1975.

Warne, Colson E. *The Pullman Boycott of 1894: The Problem of Federal Intervention*, Heath, 1955.

Wicker, Tom, "The Men in D Yard," *Esquire*, Mach, 1975.

Women's History Study Group, *What Have Women Done?* United Front Press, 1975

Yu, Connie Young, "Golden Spike's Unsung Heroes," *San Francisco Examiner*, May 10, 1969.